DARE

TO

DREAM

DEVELOP THE COURAGE AND TOOLS TO REALIZE HIGH STAKE DREAMS

LOWELL SHEPPARD

ADVANCE PRAISE

"One would imagine that, after leaving his mark in the business and agency development world, Lowell Sheppard would be thinking about taking it easy. That is not the case. In his engaging book, *Dare to Dream*, he shares details on the inner compass that drive a person to chase his dreams, no matter how rough the seas may be."
Alfonso Asensio, author, *World Wide Data*
and *Chief Kickboxing Officer*

"*Dare to Dream* is about a willingness to grow, to overcome and adventure beyond the immediate horizon. It shows the reader how to overcome self-imposed limits and push through the fortress of discomfort to achieve the impossible... or at least the unlikely. With years of experience leading and adventuring under his belt, Lowell Sheppard's message inspires those who wish to be storm riders, rather than being buffeted by the winds of change. Buy this book! It's cheaper than a pot of coffee and much more nourishing for the soul."
Jim Weisser, serial entrepreneur, Tokyo, Japan

Published by
LID Publishing
An imprint of LID Business Media Ltd.
LABS House, 15-19 Bloomsbury Way,
London, WC1A 2TH, UK

info@lidpublishing.com
www.lidpublishing.com

A member of:

BPR
businesspublishersroundtable.com

© Lowell Sheppard, 2023
© LID Business Media Limited, 2023

Printed by Severn, Gloucester
ISBN: 978-1-911687-90-0
ISBN: 978-1-911687-91-7 (ebook)

Cover and page design: Caroline Li

DARE
TO
DREAM

DEVELOP THE COURAGE AND TOOLS TO REALIZE HIGH STAKE DREAMS

LOWELL SHEPPARD

MADRID | MEXICO CITY | LONDON
BUENOS AIRES | BOGOTA | SHANGHAI

CONTENTS

This book is written
in memory of my mother.
Greta Mae Sheppard
1929 – 2023.

INTRODUCTION

I believe in the principles and rules outlined in the pages that follow. They help me realize my dreams and audacious goals. Many people abandon their dreams and ambitions due to the pressures of life, which crowd those dreams out. I believe that you, and I, can recapture those dreams and live a rich and satisfying life. I want to inspire you with real-life stories. These are lessons I have learned. Against the backdrop of my latest project, they are critical in keeping me alive – in more ways than one.

In Part One, I tell my story. I did not get a good start in life. When I showed signs of a speech impediment, the doctor told my parents, using the disparaging vernacular of the day, that I was likely 'mentally retarded.' I have proven them wrong.

In Part Two, I will help you to detect and define your dream. By understanding the anatomy of your dream, you will gain the courage to truly *dare to dream* and see your desires become a reality.

Part Three contains tips and tools to help you along the way. It is all about executing a plan and making progress.

You will be surprised at how these tips and tools can trigger momentum and progress.

Part Four is a bonus section. It contains a series of stories and insights to trigger reflection on profound themes.

HOW TO READ THIS BOOK

Years ago, a wise teacher gave me great advice on how to read a book and retain its knowledge. I have abided by her advice, which has made reading books less daunting and more productive for me. She told me to read a book three times:

1. First read it from cover to cover, but earmark (turn the corner of the page) every page where you find something interesting.
2. The second time, read all the pages that you earmarked, and search for what jumped out at you the first time – then underline those passages.
3. The third time, read what you have underlined.

The main thing is to keep moving forward – don't stop. And if you need inspiration, go back to what you have found most helpful, perhaps especially in my story, and contemplate where and why it resonates with yours. This will help to fuel your courage and perhaps give you even more insight.

I aim to prove it's never too late to dare to dream. I have discovered clues to navigating fear and living with uncertainty. I have experienced the joy of having a beginner's mind, learning to take on challenges with pleasure rather than trepidation.

This book is for everyone, no matter who you are – your gender, age or location. This book can help you.

AN OPENING EXERCISE

Before we move on, I have an exercise for you. It will pay off if you do it. There are no right or wrong answers, and you may want to keep adding to your notes as you read this book and contemplate life and your purpose.

This exercise will trigger momentum – forward motion! – which is important at this early stage. Get a piece of paper and a pen or pencil, or a whiteboard and marker, and create two columns. In column one, list every dream, and every fanciful wish, you have ever had. No matter how outlandish, spectacular or impossible you felt they were, or how young you were at the time, list them all. In the second column, write down why you have not realized those dreams or goals. Be honest. The reasons may be legitimate and important. For example, perhaps one dream had to become subservient to another. Maybe it was too dangerous, or your parents didn't let you, or you couldn't afford it. Maybe you had other priorities at the time. That's fine. Write down all the reasons why you have not realized those dreams. Now, having done this exercise, set it to one side because we will come back to it later.

There are lots of people with dreams. Most will never make those dreams a reality. But some will eagerly put their feet on the ground and start walking and taking action towards their dream. You can be one of those people, and this book will help you take that first step – or, if you have stalled in realizing your dream, it will help you restart.

A favourite quote of mine is by Paul Valéry, a 19th century poet and philosopher, who is widely quoted as having written, "The best way to make your dreams come true is to wake up."

Valéry is right. The fact that you have picked up this book is evidence that you are serious about your dream.

So, if you dare to dream, read on, and make your dream come true.

MY ROUTE AROUND JAPAN SO FAR
(OCTOBER 2023)

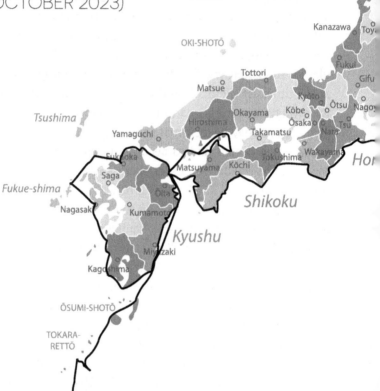

Liancourt Rocks

Sᴏ
Sᵢ

Kanazawa   Toy

OKI-SHOTŌ

Tottori   Fukui

Matsue   Gifu

Tsushima   Kyōto Ōtsu Nagoy
              Okayama Kōbe
              Hiroshima Ōsaka Tsu
Yamaguchi   Nara
              Takamatsu
Fukue-shima   Tokushima   Wakayama
Fukuoka   Matsuyama Kōchi   Hor
Saga
Nagasaki   Ōita   Shikoku
Kumamoto
              Kyushu
         Miyazaki
Kagoshima

ŌSUMI-SHOTŌ

TOKARA-
RETTŌ

AMAMI-
SHOTŌ

OKINAWA-
SHOTŌ
Naha

DAITŌ-
SHOTŌ

N A M P Ō - S H O T Ō

BONIN
ISLANDS

PART
ONE

MEMOIRS OF A MISFIT DREAMER:

HOW A 'NEVER-IN-A-MILLION-YEARS' BELIEVER BECAME A 'NEVER-TOO-LATER'

PROLOGUE

Trapped at the helm due to a broken autohelm and having had no sleep for 24 hours, I was fighting to stay awake amid a raging storm, surfing four-metre waves and avoiding ships. To be frank, I was more than a tad scared, the situation not helped by the fact I was cold and wet in spite of my foul-weather gear. With rogue waves washing over the boat and filling the cockpit with water, I was desperately trying to heed the advice an old seadog had offered me just days before.

I had moved up the date of my solo crossing of the Pacific Ocean by three years. The reason was my mother, living in Canada. I wanted to see her, and air travel was difficult and undesirable at the height of the Covid-19 pandemic. So, I prepared myself and the boat to cross the Pacific Ocean solo, starting in Japan. But first, I planned a five- to seven-day stress-test sail from Tokyo to Okinawa.

It was on that trip that I met Taro Takahashi.

I met Taro in Misaki, the day after I left the Port of Tokyo for the last time. I was on board *Wahine*, my Gib'Sea 402,

a 38-year-old, 40-foot sailboat. My ship did not yet have the
necessary electronic gear installed for my ocean crossing.
However, my contract was up at the marina, so I went on
a day's sail to the port of Misaki to finish the installation
before I proceeded out of Tokyo Bay into the Pacific.

On my second morning, a man unexpectedly visited me
and asked if I wanted to see the boat he was building to
circumnavigate the world. "Of course," I said, not knowing
who he was. This was Taro, and it turned out that he was a
legendary boat designer, having designed boats for various
iterations of the America's Cup. He had also circumnavigated more than once, and here he was, 80 years old and
building another ship to do it again. I was in awe. We visited
his boatyard, and on the way back to *Wahine* I asked him for
advice. Without hesitation, he gave me the three tips:

1. Don't fall overboard.
2. Stay calm. Panic does not help.
3. When things are tough, remember that this is your
   dream. You chose to be here. So, be happy!

His words made me think, although I didn't realize how
soon they would come back to me in a critical real-life situation. But I am getting ahead of myself.

SEASON ONE:
SEEDS OF SELF-DOUBT – THE EARLY YEARS

I don't know which came first: my parents being unkindly told I was 'mentally retarded' or my falling out of a moving vehicle. I do know that both occurred when I was three years old, and the experiences triggered a nagging self-doubt and a crippling sense of fatalism.

It was 1958, and I was lost in play with my cousin Rod in the back of our family's van – the iconic Volkswagen Type 2 – unaware that our innocent play would take a terrifying turn.

We were wrestling as we usually did – good old-fashioned rough-and-tumble play, our young bodies rolling and wrestling in the cramped space of the van. As I landed against the rear door, it suddenly flipped open, sending me hurtling out onto the road. I remember the shock and fear as I felt myself spinning repeatedly, with nothing but the shattered remains of my beloved toy ukulele to cling to.

I loved Rod. Still do. During my early childhood in British Columbia, we spent many happy summers together at our grandmother's home, having adventures in the nearby forests and rivers. I admired him. While he was always a tad shorter than me, he had the build of a muscleman. I envied that. When he laughed, his broad shoulders heaved up and down with hilarity, causing his neck to disappear into his chest. It was always a delight to watch!

I knew that Rod was my grandfather's favourite. And, to be fair, he was my grandfather's first 'blood grandson.'

When Hector Ramsay married Martha – my grandmother and the single mother of two daughters, my mother being the elder – he had an instant family. He and my grandmother then had two more daughters, the first being Heather (Rod's mother) and the second Sharon.

My mother and Auntie Heather were pregnant in the same year, 1955. I beat Rod into the world by six months. I carry our grandfather's name among my own: Ramsay. However, he was actually my mother's stepdad. My mother, who felt like an outsider and a misfit, named me to link her son to the man who had married her mother. Aware of this from an early age, I contracted my mother's affliction of a misfit.

I didn't doubt that my grandfather loved us both. However, knowing that Rod was of his blood and I wasn't, I believed he loved Rod more. Nonetheless, Rod was my best friend and I enjoyed my summers with him.

Our play was intense – we would approach our fun together with a passion and intensity that would sometimes become physical. And so it was that day in our family's Volkswagen van. Long before seatbelts became the norm or legally required, Rod and I were roughhousing in the back of the van as my father drove from White Rock to our home in Crescent Beach. And then it happened. Amid the pushing and shoving and pinning down, I was flung out of the moving vehicle. I tumbled across the tarmac and rolled into the grassy ditch, clutching my ukulele.

I don't know whether I had been about to clobber Rod with the ukulele or grabbed it for security as I felt the door give way behind me. It was my 'comfort toy.' Its destruction – shattered plastic held together by strings – brought tears and distress as I lay in the ditch watching the van disappear down the road.

Meanwhile, Rod was in shock, unable to process what had happened. It wasn't until my father noticed the open door in his rear-view mirror and heard Rod's panicked cries that he and my mother realized I was missing.

My father raced back to the ditch where I lay, crying and covered in blood from the cuts and abrasions sustained in my fall. They rushed me to my grandfather's house, where he took me in his arms and prayed for my injuries to heal. But it was clear that I needed more than just prayers, and they quickly made their way to the hospital, where I received over 20 stitches.

They likely checked for a concussion, and perhaps I had one, but I was never told. Now, with my grandparents and parents gone, there is no one left to ask. I heard the story of my falling out of the van growing up, often with someone saying with a chuckle, "Ah, that's what's wrong with him!" The story and those words stuck.

Looking back on that day, I realize it was a turning point. It was a reminder that even in our most carefree moments, fate can intervene and change everything instantly. And it was a lesson I would carry with me as I embarked on a journey to overcome my feelings of being a misfit and chase my dreams, no matter how impossible they may have seemed.

That same year, the doctor alerted my parents that something was wrong with me. Using the term common in the 1950s, he said I might be 'mentally retarded.' It was not the car accident that was cited but my lack of speech development. This assessment and stigma stuck with me as I entered elementary school and was placed in special classes. Looking back through the filter of modern literature and research, I reckon I was mildly autistic, as I displayed all the symptoms.

I only uttered my first word once I was three. Well, to be fair to myself, I had my own words. My favourite was 'ish,' but others didn't understand what I meant. I spoke my first 'real' word the day my sister was dropped off for her first day of school. The family story went that because I no longer had her to interpret for me, I started to talk. My first word was 'pop.' I was thirsty.

I discovered that while I had my impairments, my interior life was rich and fast – I just couldn't express myself. My inability to speak was a constant source of frustration and isolation. I felt trapped in my own mind, with no way to express the thoughts and emotions that raced within me. To this day, the spoken word is a challenge for me. The more syllables a word has, the more stressful it is for me to speak. But I developed a remedy. I slowly run an image of the text I want to speak across the 'screen' of my mind, and I read it. In this way, I run words through my mind like a filmstrip, slowly decoding their meaning and piecing them together.

Despite my struggles, I was a determined child, usually quiet but often obstinate and eventually rebellious. I was considered the problem child of the family. Finally, my parents, unable to understand or cope with my differences, left me with my grandmother for three months while they went on an extended overseas trip. When they returned, my mother scooped me up in maternal love, but I cried at this stranger grabbing me. I often heard my mother talk with regret about how she had left me behind.

I was eventually diagnosed as having a 'learning disability.' But I didn't need a label to know that I was different – a misfit. I felt like an outsider. And one thing was certain: I thought I was not in control of my life.

SEASON TWO:
AWAKENED
BY A MIDNIGHT
DREAM

I was fearful on my first day of school. With dread, I clutched my mother's hand as we walked under the canopy of the giant oak tree that separated the car park from the small white wooden school building in White Rock. The ground was strewn with acorns, and I felt their texture on my feet. The sound of them being shuffled and displaced accented the apprehension. I have no recollection of that school except for sitting by myself with no other students near – I have no memories of the other students. All I recall is being told I was in a 'special class.' It was a tiny room, and I was the only one there.

My solitary education ended when we moved to Regina, Saskatchewan, a few months later. Our home was a small brown stucco bungalow on Cameron Street across from Lakeview Elementary School. Lakeview was a much larger school than the one in White Rock. It was a two-storey, red-brick building surrounded by a vast playground and a chain-link fence. I have only two memories – both of feeling embarrassed and being made a spectacle.

The first was being told to stand facing the hallway wall during recess as punishment. I struggle to remember the infraction that resulted in the discipline. It did involve someone else, who was standing alongside me. I felt humiliated and scared as students rushed from the classrooms outside for a break past my co-offender and me. It was a hallway of shame, and I felt utterly humiliated, bewildered and fearful of the principal, who I discovered that day could wield power over me.

The second incident was entirely of my own doing.

The winters in Regina are harsh – well, they were when I was young, back in the 1960s. One frigid day, likely –40 degrees Farenheit or colder, I tried to lick the frost off the chain-link fence surrounding the school. As you can guess, my tongue froze to the fence. Recess ended but I was stuck, unable to move. I had no idea what to do except to risk tearing my tongue out of my mouth by exerting one mighty pull by pushing my feet against the fence. Minutes passed as I tried to summon the courage and the will to dislodge my tongue with brute force, when a man outside the fence saw my predicament. His face remains anonymous, but the appearance of his large furry gloves enveloping my face, mouth and tongue was welcomed. Bringing his mouth close to mine, he blew hot air onto my tongue, capturing and retaining the heat with his gloves. It took several blows, but eventually the ice that had joined my tongue to the fence melted, and I was freed. I was also relieved and filled with gratitude towards the stranger. I hurried off back inside the school, feeling foolish having become the center of attention for a number of passers-by watching.

Thankfully, I escaped the shame caused by both incidents at the school and in the neighbourhood when we moved to a new house a mile away and I was enrolled at Wascana Primary School.

Despite my lack of confidence and being awkward socially, academically and in most sports, my imagination and dreams were vivid. It was at our new house, when I was aged ten, that I was woken by one such dream that unsettled me. Perhaps because it seemed so real. Or maybe because it was spiritual in texture. But also, because it touched a nerve deep within me, triggering thoughts of desire and ambition, giving me a glimpse of what my life could be, as if I now had a view beyond the parapet that had blocked my vision of myself and the future.

There are elements of the dream that I still hesitate to share in detail, but suffice to say it was set in my back yard in Regina. I was suddenly lifted up and out of the confines of that yard and then, with a bird's eye view, I saw the world below me. I soared over oceans, mountains, deserts and more. At the risk of overstating its gravitas, in which I am no doubt influenced by my missionary family upbringing, the dream had a 'sense of calling' tone, where my destiny and purpose were somehow to change the world. I was exhilarated, and then I woke up. Bursting into tears, I ran into my parents' bedroom. Looking back, I can see that I was conflicted.

The dream was exciting yet at the same time debilitating. On the one hand, such was the power of the dream and its message that it gave me a spark of incentive to find a way to experience the world. I could picture myself sailing across oceans, flying aeroplanes and taking on feats of endurance. But, on the other hand, the immediate effect of the dream was that it plunged me into despair and even further into the belief that I would never achieve and experience such things. I told myself these were mere fairy tales, as I didn't have the courage or know-how to pursue them. My life would be idle, and my aspirations would remain unfulfilled.

As I wrestled with this inner turmoil, and despite the odds stacked against me, I was beginning to refuse to be defined by my social, academic and physical limitations. Instead, I started to focus on how I would find my way and fulfil my destiny. The midnight dream left me with a lingering sense that my life should not be wasted.

The assessments and treatment of my impairments were few and far between. Each time I changed schools, the paperwork did not follow me, and checks and special classes resulted. One therapist told me that my upper-body strength but lack of upper-body coordination were symptomatic of a 'disorder,' as was the fact that despite having skinny legs, I had lower-body coordination. That made sense. I always felt self-conscious throwing a ball. My biceps and broad shoulders belied that I could not throw a ball properly. I just looked odd and felt self-conscious. People would comment and chuckle. But my pencil-shaped legs, while skinny, could take me anywhere and take me fast. It was the one thing that was giving me a growing sense of confidence. I could run. And I could not only run fast, but I could run further and longer than most. It was this one ounce of self-belief that I focused on. It took me as far as running in track-and-field events for the school, excelling in the 400 metres, the 800 metres and cross-country. And this belief in my legs led me to sign up for an endurance challenge at age 12 that changed my life.

The opportunity presented itself as a 35-mile walk for charity, Miles for Millions, in my hometown – by then Winnipeg, Manitoba. I signed up with my friend Doug, and to my surprise, I completed it. This experience taught or reinforced me four keys to my success that redefined my view of myself:

1. My legs were capable of taking me places, fast!
2. When you make a decision, it triggers a chain reaction. Once I had decided to take on this challenge, momentum carried me through signing up, raising sponsors, training and completing the walk.

3. Adventure is more meaningful and gratifying when it has a purpose.
4. Refuelling helps!

I unexpectedly learned the importance of refuelling four miles from the finish line.

At the 31-mile mark of the charity walk, the familiar sight of our home and the church where my father served as a minister came into view. My father had promised me a meal and a break before continuing on, but what I hadn't expected was the act of humility and service that he would perform.

As we sat to eat, my father brought out a basin of warm water and soap and removed my shoes and socks, washing my feet with tender care. The memory of that moment is still etched in my mind. But what I found especially impactful was what he said next.

Seeing how tired his 12-year-old son was becoming, he said, "Well done, son! You've walked 31 miles. No need to do more. We're proud of you."

I responded with a resolute, "No way, Dad. I'm going to finish this walk."

Ninety minutes later, I called my dad from a payphone, triumphantly declaring, "Dad, I did it!"

It changed me. A light went on. I could endure, experience adventure and help others all at the same time. While the chronic feeling of being different remained, it dimmed in the light of the glow of my achievement. I was on to something. My life would never be the same again. The dream I'd had at age ten, which remained vivid, was no longer a pipe dream, never to be realized. Instead, my inner world was now large and less restrained by the anchors of past self-doubt.

SEASON THREE:
FINDING MY
SUPERPOWER

Growing up, I couldn't shake off my wanderlust. My parents, who were always on the move as my father was a travelling minister, had instilled the same desire for adventure and discovery in me. We travelled across Canada and the USA in a cramped nine-metre airstream trailer, and in other countries we stayed in people's homes. But I still felt confined. I dreamed of flying aeroplanes, crossing deserts and sailing across oceans.

In my early teens, I was introduced to dinghy sailing. It quickly became my escape, my way to dream of adventure and freedom. I spent my nights on the narrow floor of the trailer, dreaming of sailing, and during the day I sketched sailboats. As I grew older, I discovered the thrill of sailing fast dinghies, known as lasers. I revelled in sailing the laser to the risk of capsizing. Loved it. With my feet secured by straps, my abs got a great workout as I lay horizontal with my butt over the edge of the boat and dunked my head into the waves. All day long I would practise righting the dinghy when it tipped over, with one easy continuous motion of climbing, leveraging my weight on the upturned keel, and walking myself out of the water into the cockpit as the boat rolled and the keel became the platform from which I could 'step' back into the dinghy. I was thrilled every time I practised the manoeuvre.

And then there was flying. But it was expensive and, as a teenager, I had not built up any savings. However, I firmly believed in the idea that 'where there is a will, there is a way,' so I took two jobs to pay for it. I worked full time at a ply-wood mill on the 'green chain,' which was where the wood came 'wet' into the mill. I changed shifts every two weeks, alternating between daytime (8 am to 4 pm) and afternoon (4 pm to midnight) shifts. My other job was at Vancouver International Airport, in the exit booth of the car park, working the graveyard shift from 12:30 am to 7:30 am. It was only minutes from the mill, but even without needing to travel between the two jobs I was working 16-hour days to pay for my flying lessons.

More than once, I fell asleep in the booth and was woken by blaring horns as a queue of cars quickly formed with pas-sengers who had arrived on a red-eye flight and were eager to get home to bed themselves. But it was worth it, as it meant I could afford more flying hours, putting me on the fast track to my first solo flight.

There is nothing quite like the sheer joy and the sense of freedom and accomplishment of soloing for the first time. My opportunity came unexpectedly. After an hour of train-ing in the Cessna 150, and after we had taxied back to the hangar, the instructor jumped out and ordered me to do a circuit on my own. I didn't wait to confirm I had heard him right. I said "OK," and once he was clear, I taxied back to the runaway, getting clearance from air traffic control to take off. I danced the wings of the aeroplane in celebration! As I landed and taxied back to the hangar, my face already in a broad smile, I beamed when I heard the air traffic controller congratulate me on my first solo flight against the applause in the background of the other controllers in the air traffic control tower.

Eventually, I took some college courses and got a job at a local newspaper. But what I really wanted to do was to fly.

So, when I was in my early twenties and an opportunity arose to go to Mexico and fly with an aviation mission as a second pilot, I leaped at the opportunity. Flying as second pilot meant that I could log those hours in my pilot logbook and gain more experience. I was working for a non-governmental organization (NGO) that flew doctors and dentists to remote villages. But I was also assigned other tasks that included beekeeping and working on a farm. These small businesses helped to finance the aviation mission. It was an adrenaline-filled year flying onto remote mountain airstrips as the second pilot and landing on rough runaways, one of which was on a slope high in the mountains and L-shaped. It was daring and exciting, but when I returned to Canada, my desire to fly was satisfied. I had done it – no need to continue. But the dream of sailing continued.

One of my pilot friends in Vancouver, Doug Hoffman, owned a Yamaha 26 sailboat. He took me out a couple of times and then let me sail it on my own. I loved it and would often take it out in storms to test the boat and my limits. It also became a fun way of dating a pretty young lady, Kande, who was later to become my wife.

I retained the quiet and relatively private demeanour I had developed as a child. I thought more than I talked – but no longer because I felt like a misfit. Instead it was because I had so many dreams and visions and desires that I wanted to stay focused, and it was wonderfully satisfying for me to think, plan and even scheme – and most of all imagine everything that I wanted to do.

I began to discover powerful principles that, although common in some ways, became superpowers for me when I tapped into them and applied them. Some derived from my father, but others were firm conclusions I had reached. These superpowers were such a discovery for me, and gave me such an intense sense of exhilaration, that it was as if I thought I was the first person ever to discover them.

It wasn't until recently that I saw someone else describe one of these principles as a superpower. I was reading *Four Thousand Weeks* by Oliver Burkeman, a British author who writes that the ability to endure discomfort with a long-term goal in mind is a superpower.[1] "Yes!" I declared to myself. "He is right. I have proven it to be so. Perseverance!"

I continued to find that old adage true: 'Where there is a will, there is a way.' And I discovered an action sequence that allowed me to put it into practice. The sequence is:

- Visualization
- Choice
- Vocalization
- Perseverance
- Beginner's mind

This season of my life was one of growth, self-actualization, for sure, and glimpses of what the future could be.

SEASON FOUR:
FACING DEATH AND MYSTERY

Entering adult life, I took on responsibilities as a husband, father and leader of various organizations, each bringing its challenges. The residual self-doubt was never far from the surface of my consciousness, but I was developing coping techniques.

My 'speech impediment,' as my teachers called it in junior high school, continued. The slightest stress worsened it. I faced it head-on when I started public speaking. Some bolder people would comment on my peculiar pronunciation of words. It always embarrassed me, but I did not stop trying to refine my abilities. My work in the non-profit sector took me to many places including war zones and areas of famine and natural disasters. I had good mentors who passed on their values to me. I was learning that helping others means truly putting others first.

Kande and I moved continents twice, first to England as a young couple and then to Japan as a young family. Moving places is exhilarating and is an opportunity to awaken the beginner's mind.

While I tried to follow in my father's footsteps and for a time was an interim minister at a small church in the Gulf Islands, I realized that parish work was not for me because I lacked patience with people. Also, I was increasingly influenced by a particular theology that focused on the here and now rather than the hereafter. But most important, if I'm being honest with myself, was a discovery that I was predisposed to doubt rather than belief.

This intellectual disposition, combined with the cultural influences of my generation (flower power, 'make love, not war,' etc.) were shaping my values and life trajectory.

Over the following years and decades, three significant incidents pushed, shoved and cajoled me to rethink my life:

1. The first was acquiring a bicycle shortly after moving to Japan.
2. The second was the triple disaster of 2011 in Japan.
3. The third was nearly dying twice in 2012.

But first I need to explain how I ended up in Japan. The reason was a deal I had with Kande.

She had been born and raised in Japan, the daughter of missionaries. When we were married in Vancouver in 1980 – after a courtship that took place partly on the water and partly on land – we agreed that if she would move with me to the UK, where I wanted to live, one day I would move with her to Japan. In 1996, she said it was time to fulfil my side of the bargain. In moving to Japan, I assumed that my dream to live on a sailboat and cross an ocean would never be realized – Japan was just too expensive, and my language skills were rudimentary. So instead, I threw myself into writing books and took up a new challenge, long-distance bike-riding, including making an epic 3,000 km bike ride the length of Japan in the year 2000 (more on this in

"Season Five" below). I also founded an NGO called HOPE International Development Agency Japan.

Life was gratifying. I used cycling to raise money to help impoverished families gain access to clean water. It was simply amazing how their lives were transformed with a little bit of help from others and a whole lot of determination and innovation on their part to leverage the gift of clean water to gain better health, housing and education.

Then over two successive years, life became intense and I came close to death – twice.

2011,
WHEN THE EARTH SHOOK
AND THE SEA ROSE

In 2011, my world, and the archipelago I had come to call home, were shaken – literally – by a triple disaster: the Great East Japan Earthquake and resulting tsunami, combined with the Fukushima nuclear disaster.

Initially, I focused on ensuring HOPE was doing all it could for the region hardest hit by the earthquake and tsunami, following our usual procedures. But I still remember the words of Harry Hill, the president of one of our most prominent supporters, Oak Lawn Marketing. He asked what HOPE would do in response to the tsunami to help with the rebuilding effort. When I said nothing, he asked why. I said it was because rebuilding was outside our mandate. And to this Harry replied, "We are all outside our mandate – this is our community, and we all must step in and help." He was right.

Oak Lawn Marketing deposited $1 million into HOPE's bank account, with a further $1.5 million being donated by the firm's three principals and suppliers. With the generosity of Robert Roche, Tadashi Nakamura and Harry Hill – and the companies they bought from and were in partnerships with, including NTT Docomo – we saw over 20 communities get back on their feet, with 70 companies helped to start up or restart their operations.

Days after the earthquake, Harry and I flew up the spine of Japan in a helicopter organized by our friend Chris Glenn to assess the damage. Unlike earthquake preparedness, the planning for a tsunami had been patchy. It was noteworthy how the exceedingly strong earthquake caused little damage (with credit to the building codes in Japan), yet the tsunami destroyed extensive stretches of coastline and reached up to 10 km inland in some places – at a terrific and terrible human cost. This was an intense time, and it took a toll on me physically and mentally.

CLOSE CALLS WITH DEATH

While 2011 diverted my professional and even emotional attention to northeast Japan, it was 2012 that forever altered my view of myself and the future.

It was a stressful year for everyone in Japan, myself included, as the country was still reeling from the triple disaster. Enabled by the generous donation of Oak Lawn Marketing, we were seeing the effects of our aid distribution and economic development support, which was satisfying. But, against the backdrop of this success, I had my own triple disaster, two instances of which were life-threatening.

In April, I contracted dengue fever and was laid up for six weeks. Then in July, while preparing to cycle, I was stung by a bee, went into anaphylactic shock and was unconscious within four minutes. Fortunately, due to the quick thinking of my youngest son Mackenzie and the skilful driving of my wife, I was treated and 'brought back' in the intensive care unit of a local hospital.

A month later, I developed pain in my leg that turned out to be a blood clot that had travelled into my lungs. It was only discovered when, after I had been limping for two weeks, my daughter-in-law, Maria, insisted I go to a hospital to be checked. After a series of tests including a CAT scan, I was told that I had a deep vein thrombosis and a pulmonary embolism and mustn't move. I spent the next ten days in hospital being treated.

My family, friends and colleagues all warned me to be careful in the future, travel less and be outside less. I must confess I was a little shaken by the experience but was liberated by an admonishment from my friend David McKenzie, who advised me, "Lowell, it's better to die doing something than die doing nothing."

That was it. I was back on the bike in no time with an EpiPen dangling from my hip and blood thinners in my bag.

SEASON FIVE:
FROM BIKES TO BOATS – RETIREMENT IS NOT AN OPTION

Crossing the Atlantic at age 15 on a cruise liner birthed in me the fanciful idea of crossing the ocean in a sailboat one day. The North Atlantic – then the only ocean I knew – captivated me with its challenge and allure.

After a year of travelling in Europe, my father decided that instead of going home to Canada by plane, we would sail on the *Empress of Canada*, a Canadian-owned cruise liner. He wanted to relive his transatlantic crossing on the *Queen Mary* in 1949, on which he had met the Crown Prince of Japan (who would later become emperor), with whom he had discussed spirituality and faith. I still have the letter written by the Crown Prince's private secretary on his behalf, to my father on paper with the *Queen Mary*'s letterhead.

In April 1970 we boarded the *Empress of Canada* in Liverpool, sailed past Ireland and experienced a relatively calm crossing of the Atlantic, eventually passing New-foundland, entering the St Lawrence Seaway and dock-ing in Montreal. The voyage enchanted me. It was not so much the onboard entertainment, although that was fun and memorable. What made more of an impression on me was standing on deck and gazing during the day into the endless grey of the Atlantic and at night into the infinite sky. Midnight was particularly significant as it lasted one hour to adjust to the change in time zone. Time stood still. It felt magical to me.

But my youthful dream of sailing across an ocean was a distant thought when I moved to Japan in 1996. What captured my imagination shortly after moving to the land of Kande's birth was using a bicycle as my primary means of transportation. I had grown up riding bicycles as most youngster do. But it had mostly been a way to get around the neighbourhood quickly. Shortly after moving to Japan, I acquired a mountain bike and fell in love with exploring further and further from home. Eventually I would do cross-country day trips, clocking up 50–80 km on a ride. It was during cherry blossom season one year that I came up with the idea of riding my bike the length of Japan, about 3,000 km, to follow the annual cherry blossom front that sweeps the country, triggering outdoor flower-viewing parties for the fleeting few days that the blossom season lasts. Riding a bike was about the perfect speed I thought. Happily a publisher in the UK liked the idea and I was given a book contract to write about the trip in the deep travel genre. The advance they gave me paid for me to get a bicycle made, and it also funded my expenses along the way. It was exciting but also daunting.

EPIC BIKE RIDE:
A LIFE-CHANGER

It is no exaggeration to say that this bike ride changed my life.

For two years prior, I fell asleep every night fretting, planning and dreaming about it. As I trained for the ride, the bike became part of my life. I often got up before sunrise and rode 50–100 km before breakfast. The ride itself transformed me. It increased my confidence and physical and mental well-being, and in fact I went on to do many more bike rides after the cherry blossom ride: I entered triathlons and races, and loved them. Cycling became a beautiful part of my life.

On the final day of the cherry blossom ride, I reflected on my life and how the ride had changed me. This is what I wrote:

> The forest was quiet around me, and my spirit and mind became one, and I wandered into my thoughts. It was the last day of travelling alone, and I felt the inner glow of knowing I had achieved my goal. Then it came, as clear as a whisper in a quiet room. It was a moment spiritual in content and texture but unaccompanied by anything dramatic or supernatural. There was no booming voice from the sky, yet the words that came brought extraordinary clarity unlocking residual self-doubt. They went as a caboose at the end of a train of thought. As fleeting as the moment was, like the cherry blossoms, the words could not have come with such power and healing without the six weeks of pedalling and pain that had gone before. It was a profoundly private moment, but I knew I had cycled the length of Japan for those words.[2]

Since then, I have had many bicycle and physical adventures. I rode my bike across Cambodia three times, on the third going through the Cardamom Mountains and tiger country. Each time I led a group of cyclists who were raising money for HOPE. There were also hill races, triathlons and several Japan coast-to-coast rides: Japan at its widest, Japan at its narrowest, Japan at its stormiest and once the long way around with my dog! My good friends Mark McBennett and Tony Torres rode with me on my first coast-to-coast and together we organized the subsequent ones.

The third of these coast-to-coast trips was meant to be a pleasant ride from the Sea of Japan to the Pacific, arriving in time for a bicycle festival in the tsunami zone sponsored by Cannondale. But, in the end, it took me and my friend Stuart Ayre three attempts to make it over the mountain range. The first two passes we rode up to were closed or washed out near the top. Each attempt required about 20 km of uphill slog through wind and rain from the valley floor of Yamagata Prefecture, only to find we had to turn back, descend the valley and cycle 20–30 km further until we found another road to another pass. All the while, sponsors could watch our progress via a live tracker. One sponsor, Nick Johnston, texted me as he was watching us go up and down and then up again and down again in the storm, which he could see on CNN. His text contained a word and a pledge. The word was "RESPECT." The pledge was to increase his sponsorship tenfold from $100 to $1,000.

I enjoyed and benefitted from all these challenges, but none was as transformative and spiritual in texture as the cherry blossom bike ride had been. I was hungry to experience something big again – something audacious, significant and risky. Something that would fill my dreams as I slept, and capture and focus my thoughts while I was awake. I assumed it would again involve a bike. However, when I returned to sailing, a dormant dream was reactivated.

REDISCOVERING SAILING

As I've mentioned, I had given up on my childhood dream of owning a sailboat, living on her and crossing an ocean on her. Japan just seemed too expensive.

Then I discovered two sets of sailors. One group was Japanese and introduced to me by Nakashima san, a volunteer with HOPE. She had a friend, Yajima-san, who had become a HOPE supporter. Yajima-san owned two small sailboats and invited me to go sailing. Around the same time, I discovered the Tokyo Sail and Power Squadron (TSPS). In Japan, you need a boat operator's licence to operate a boat with an engine over 2 hp. I had inquired about this before but had been put off because the course cost thousands of dollars and the exam was in Japanese. But the TSPS offered English lessons that cost only a few hundred dollars, and by special arrangement they offered the course in English. I took the course and passed my Class 2 Licence, which allowed me to operate up to a 20-tonne boat within five nautical miles of the shore. These two connections opened my eyes to the sailing world in Japan. I realized that it was less expensive and opaque than I thought.

So, I started to sail again. And then it came – with the reawakening of a dream came a goal, a challenge and a plan that would give life to the dream and a reason to make it a reality. It came in the night, the time of dreams. It woke me, and I shuddered, and I could not get it out of my head.

REAWAKENED DREAM

Some dreams and goals are immediately robust and sturdy. You can blurt them out, and you know, and everyone around you thinks or even says, boldly, "Yep, that will happen!"

Other dreams are fragile and require nurture and careful consideration. Such was the case with this one: to cross the Pacific solo before I was 70 (I was then 63).

So, for a time, I had to talk to myself about the idea before I shared it with anyone. I had to ask myself questions and do some soul-searching. Did I really want this, given its high stakes? Could I do it? And was there a reasonable path forward to realize it?

This was it. And it was scary.

My dream was to buy a boat, live on her and sail across an ocean. More specifically, my goal was to buy a boat soon, learn how to sail her and cross the North Pacific solo before I was 70. In an inner conversation with myself I was questioning whether I was serious.

I slowly began to share my plan with my family, then select friends and some in the sailing community. While they expressed surprise and asked good questions, their acceptance strengthened my desire and resolved to do it.

THE PLAN

This was autumn 2018. As I entered 2019, I sent out invitations to my 64th birthday party in March. In the invitation, I said I would make three announcements on my birthday and wanted the invitees to be present. There was much speculation about those three announcements, and it was fun keeping people in suspense.

Finally, the day arrived. About 70 people gathered in Tokyo and a further 50 people in Nagoya a few days later.

The three announcements were that I was going to:

1. Find someone to succeed me in my role running HOPE.
2. Return to speaking and writing.
3. Buy a boat and cross the Pacific solo before I was 70.

Four years earlier, I'd had an epiphany about my retirement.

When I turned 60, people began to talk about my retirement. Friends and family inquired what I wanted to do, and colleagues asked me what my succession plan was. While I did not mind the conversations, I did not welcome them either.

The epiphany occurred in the rear of an aircraft returning from a donor visit to HOPE's project area in Cambodia. Having been moved once again by the tenacity and grit of impoverished families who could attain self-reliance with just a little help from others, I determined never to retire. We are all unique and positioned to accomplish things, change and affect things that no one else can. Yes, skills and relationships can be acquired, but there is only one you, and you have a responsibility to be you.

So, in the cheap seats at the back of the aeroplane (the donor was in business class), I resolved never to retire and instead to continue working hard to make a difference from my particularly unique position in life.

I had to tell my family. I did it household by household, starting with Kande and moving on to my sons and extended family. When I told my son Ryan and his wife Maria, a seal was put on my decision. I told them over dinner, during which my grandson Eli was playing on the floor beside me. He was two years old. Near the end of the meal, I said to Ryan and Maria, "I am not doing this for you. I am doing it for him – Eli and his generation." At that point, Eli leaned into my chest, hugged me and said, "Thank you, Gwampa." From that point, I was committed and obligated. I still tingle thinking about that moment.

That tingling feeling is essential. It means that whatever thought has run through your head has stimulated your emotion and desire, and you will be able to draw on that power when things get tough. Dreams are rooted in selfishness – a deep desire. Passion is more than casual curiosity. Being inquisitive is excellent and vital in discovering your goals. But more is needed to propel you forward into the storm and challenging times. I remembered and drew on the tingling feeling as I considered my plan and made the big step of announcing it at my birthday.

When the thought of crossing the Pacific solo before I was 70 first came to me, I was unsure but also deeply curious, which resulted in me reaching deep into myself to ask why. Why did I want to do this? What I discovered surprised me and remained at the core of my motivation as I trained and prepare for the crossing. It was in the process of reaching into myself, before I allowed anyone else into my secret desire, that I discovered the why. While crossing an ocean was exciting and daunting and arriving in Vancouver would be extraordinary, the real reason I wanted to do it was to find a place of solitude, even if I only experienced it for a few moments. This place of solitude ultimately became real for me, and I have come to call it Nemo North.

Nemo North is the sacred notion of being in a place where only you and life's most profound questions exist.

Nemo North now has a set of actual coordinates. It is the name I have given to the North Pacific equivalent of Point Nemo, the place in the South Pacific that is the furthest from land in any direction on earth. Google it yourself to read more about Point Nemo, its discovery and its mysteries. I narrowed down my search for Nemo North using a tip from Marian Marx. Now, with the help of TSPS fellow member Nemanja Komatinovic, I have the precise coordinates:

37°58'45.13"N
148°1'12.17"W

In his *Critique of Practical Reason* (1788) Immanuel Kant referred to two things that strike us with reverence and awe: looking up and looking within. I have added a third. My three are looking up to the expanse above, within to the mysteries of the soul and below to the terrors of the deep. Nemo North represents that place for me.

And this is against the backdrop of a very social life. I always dreaded being alone – well, I would sometimes find being with people exhausting, but the alone times could be terrifying. That was why I wanted to go to Nemo North – to face that fear. This is exceedingly quirky, I know, and many don't get it. But it remained for me the most critical aspect of my dream: to face that fear authentically.

But there were other motivations too: to bring attention to the oceans, to illustrate to my grandson that adventures can have a purpose and to leave a legacy.

WHEN I TURNED 64

And so it was. A dream was reawakened, a goal was set and plans were being made. Before my birthday announcements, I put together a plan. Although my life was comfortable enough, I knew I couldn't afford this dream. I had spent a life in the non-profit sector but now I needed a mountain of cash. By a bit of a fluke on a land detail – and from partly building our house ourselves – Kande and I had a unique solar-powered log house on a mountainside in the city of Seto, just outside Nagoya. But I promised Kande that I would not put the home at risk (it was primarily mortgaged anyway) and that I would find alternative means to finance my dream.

So with pen and paper, I wrote down the name of the project and my plan. To my surprise, the name Pacific Solo was not taken, and I could grab the URL with the help of my friend Bruce, who runs a website support business. Naively I thought a YouTube channel would help me create some income so I started the Pacific Solo channel with the help of my filmmaker friend Ryan Seale. Ryan also helped to create a brand around Pacific Solo, and so it was with a nice-looking logo that I went to my 64th birthday party to announce my plans. By that point I realized that this could not be a hobby – it had to be a business for it to be sustainable.

At my birthday party, I made the three announcements. Many had not seen them coming and there was an audible gasp when I spoke about Pacific Solo. The other two announcements were that it was time for someone else to take over the leadership of HOPE and that I was going to return to speaking and writing with a particular focus on sustainability, goal-setting and leaving a lasting social legacy. I planned to found a new consultancy called Navigate 22. That business would eventually morph into Never Too Late – but more on that later.

I went into overdrive in my planning. I had much to do, including officially resigning from my position at HOPE, activating the search for a successor with the board and continuing to launch the Pacific Solo website, Facebook page and YouTube channel. And most importantly of all, I begin my search for sponsors. I expected 2020 to be the year everything came together, but things moved faster than I expected, and then an unexpected virus threw in a curve ball.

By the time of my birthday announcements in late March 2019, I had already begun a quiet search for a boat. I had two lines of enquiry. One was with a small search team I had set up in Japan within the Japanese sailing community. It was made up of Nakashima san as a translator; Yajima-san, for whom I was occasional crewing; and Yamashita-san, a boat broker in Tokyo. The second line of enquiry was with two of my acquaintances in Phuket, Thailand. Gary and Dagmar were a dynamic couple who owned boats and ran a boat brokerage out of Hong Kong. Gary invited me to Thailand to see several boats and at least learn about buying a boat.

Three weeks before my birthday, Kande and I went to Phuket. None of the boats was suitable, but we left having learned a lot. Gary mentored me. He stressed that there is no perfect boat, that we would want a composite of the things we liked in all the boats we visited, and that I would know which boat was for me because she would speak to me. The last of these might seem strange, but it made sense to me. In the wake of my father's death, I had longed for a border collie; when I found her, we had made eye contact and the dog had spoken to me.

It is irrational to anthropomorphize a boat, but it is common practice.

I returned to Japan and continued the search. In April, I convened my Japanese search team for the second time

on Yamashita-san's boat (a Grand Banks MotorYacht). During our meeting, Yamashita-san told me of a boat on the
neighbouring dock that was for sale that happened to be
owned by a foreigner. In fact, I had taken a stroll down that
dock before and stopped to glance at that same boat a few
weeks ago. Yamashita-san contacted the owner through a
fellow broker and arranged a viewing and sea trial for the
following week. She spoke to me and has been speaking to
me ever since. She is a Gib'Sea 402, built in 1988 in France –
a boat with beautiful lines and a low profile yet exceptional
headroom below. I had shortlisted a handful of boats by
this time, but all were far off. This one was in the marina
where I wanted to be based initially. The marina is called
Yumenoshima, which means 'Island of Dreams.' Critically,
it is just minutes from central Tokyo and my small apartment that I had there because of my frequent business trips.
Sailing a boat to Tokyo was an option, but it would have
been difficult because there was a two-year waiting list for
a berth. This boat was already there.

Following the sea trial, I felt confident that the boat was
for me, but there was a big problem. Finding her was prema-
ture as I needed more money. Two things had to happen: I
had to cash in a small private pension, which would take
months, and I needed to raise some sponsorship money.
One sponsor, UFC Gym Japan, had already stepped forward, and I was talking to others, but I needed more as I
hadn't expected to buy a boat so soon. The owner, Marcus,
was eager to sell and offered me an interest-free loan for six
months to give me time. So, I signed the agreement and took
possession on 1 July 2019. Tokyo Supercars soon stepped
in and became one of my first two sponsors together with
UFC Gym Japan. Ultimately, after a little nail-biting and a
lot of bureaucracy, I cashed my pension in two weeks before
the six months ran out and paid Marcus on time.

There was much to do and learn, including terminating the contract on my small Tokyo apartment, moving on board, learning to get in and out of the dock and changing the boat's name. Each was a process, but changing the boat's name was the most troublesome.

For some months, I had cogitated over what to name the boat that I would eventually buy. I went through several phases of thought.

When I initially envisaged sailing solo across the Pacific by the time I was 70, my first thought was to use the term of endearment my father had used for my mother: Mildred. Yes... my father was a romantic soul. I wanted to honour my mother and father, and I wanted my mother to have the pleasure of seeing me name the boat after her.

But the harsh reality of finding the finances to buy the boat sunk in. Life in the NGO world has been hugely rewarding and satisfying in many ways, but not with zeroes in the bank account. So, I initially decided to sell the naming rights to the boat to a sponsor to raise cash.

But, try as I might, the decision just didn't sit right with me. One morning I woke up and said, "Damn! It will be my boat, and I want to name it!"

I was then advised, and it seemed to make sense, that as the boat would serve as a metaphor and motif for Navigate22 (the ethics, sustainability and social legacy consultancy that was part of my plan), the boat should bear the same name as the company. So the name *NAV22* was being considered, and I even began to look at some possible logos. But that idea quickly led to the conclusion that the boat should bear the name of the great adventure she and I would have – *Pacific Solo*.

I wrote *Pacific Solo* as the name of the boat on the document I submitted to transfer the registration from Marcus to myself.

But again the decision nagged at me. This was partly because of my research, which had revealed the importance of rituals in the marine world, where de-naming a boat (an act of blasphemy after which one must appease the gods) and naming a ship (a sacred action requiring divine blessings) required special rituals. Then, in discovering the significance of names for boats, it struck me. I was not the new owner of the boat! I was merely the new custodian. So, out of respect for the vessel and all who had sailed her, I retained her name: *Wahine*, which is Polynesian for 'woman.'

On 27 June 2019, I became her legal guardian.

And so began my relationship with SV *Wahine*.

She was the largest boat I had sailed to date, and the former first mate gave me some valuable lessons on leaving and entering the dock. He taught me angles and different approaches, considering tidal current and wind direction. It was the first time I heard the term 'prop walk.' Every boat is different. The angle of the blades and whether they spin clockwise or counter-clockwise will determine the direction of the prop walk when a boat is in reverse. On *Wahine*, the boat goes straight forward but the prop walk direction is to port. This is handy for docking on the port side; you can enter at up to 25–30 degrees dead slow, and when you want to stop, you engage reverse and the stern of the boat will swing into the port.

This was the beginning of learning a new lexicon for living on and operating a boat. Port and starboard (left and right) were easy, but there were many other terms and words to learn. For example, you never refer to 'rope' on a boat; once rope comes on a boat, it is called 'line,' and once that line has been put to use, it refers to something more specific. For example, lines that go up to control sails are 'halyards,' and those that are horizontal to control sails are 'sheets.' While I had sailed quite a bit on dinghies and in the Mediterranean on a 40-foot Sun Fizz with a skipper, I had never taken formal lessons. I had confidence in my acquired skill and intuition in sailing – point of wind, angle of sails, how much sail, etc. – but I needed to be more sailing-literate. My learning was just beginning, and the curve would be steep! I was about to be thrown in at the deep end in learning about gearboxes, drive shafts, diesel engines, navigation, reading the clouds and marine charts as well as all the other things that would be essential to my dream – social media management, algorithms, video editing *and* living with uncertainty!

One thing is for sure, I was a complete novice and accepted advice and training from anyone willing to offer it. I assumed that everyone knew more than I did! It was invigorating. I soon learned that having a boat meant you always had a list of boat projects. One of my first was to replace the helm compass. My steep learning curve was complicated by the fact that *Wahine* was a French boat. The day after I legally acquired *Wahine*, electrical issues arose, and I was left with French manuals. Then, like a gust of wind, Robin and Mina Mah appeared offering assistance. Robin became an important part of my shore team and a supporter. This experience was an early indicator that despite the name 'Pacific Solo', I couldn't navigate this journey alone.

The existing one worked well enough, but the cover was glazed over, making the compass blurry, and all attempts to clean it up and make it usable again failed. I bought one that was supposed to fit. It didn't. It nearly did, but the screw holes were 22 mm off. So, I fabricated a mount, and now *Wahine* had a usable compass in the cockpit. I could see my bearing and know where I was going!

In early August, in the midst of my training, I took a couple of friends out on a day sail. On the way into the marina, I lost forward gear, and in the end I had to reverse into the dock. When *Wahine* was examined by the marina mechanic, it was revealed that the gearbox had worn out. It would require about $5,000 and three weeks on the hard (meaning out of the water on a stand).

I was shocked and worried. At this point I still owed Marcus, the previous owner, a boat-load of money, and now I had this additional cost. When I lamented my situation to a fellow boat owner, I heard for the first time the old saying that 'BOAT' stands for Bring Out Another Thousand. It was my first test of resilience and tenacity. I accepted it, authorized the expenditure and took advantage of *Wahine* being out of the water to do other things, like cleaning and painting her hull and addressing a problem I had spotted on the keel. I put out a call for help to the mailing list of *Wahine*, which I had inherited, along with some friends I had made through the TSPS. Many responded, including my TSPS instructor, Claude Staube, and David LaHeist, who had crewed on *Wahine* for Marcus.

Finally, the day arrived to put *Wahine* back in the water. It was the first week of September, and I invited my son Ryan to join me in taking Wahine out for relaxing cruise. It was a perfect day, and I revelled in being out on the water with the wind in the sail.

I slipped *Wahine* back into her slip, feeling happy and pleased. It was time to reward all those who had helped me over the summer.

Twenty-four hours later, I had ten people on board who had generously given their time and skills over the previous weeks to help repaint and repair *Wahine*. I was to take them on a thank-you cruise for a few hours. We were all ready to go: people were in their places wearing life jackets, and the lines were ready to be thrown. But I could not get into reverse gear.

I gently nudged the throttle foward, and nothing happened. Two of my shore team, Stephan and Claude went to the engine room as I worked the throttle. They reported that the engine was revving and the shaft was turning, but there was no boat movement or water churning. Stephan, an experienced sailor, said it was as if there wasn't a propeller. Another sailor, my *sempai* (mentor) Rick the TSPS, stripped down to his shorts and dove under the boat to confirm.

No propeller!

We had taken the propeller off to grind and clean it over the summer, but we had not reinstalled it properly. So when it had spun forward, it had been alright, but when I had put the boat into reverse to take advantage of the prop walk to bring the stern into the dock after the sail with Ryan, the prop had spun off. We searched for the propeller with no luck – it had disappeared into the murky, muddy depths below.

What to do? *Wahine* was an old boat made in France and parts were difficult to come by, particularly a propeller. For weeks, there seemed to be no solution.

I felt upset and wondered whether this was ongoing lousy luck or par for the course. Later that day, I went a social gathering at the Tokyo Yacht Club meeting room. The news of my losing a prop had made it before me. I was a laughing stock: without exception, other boat owners pronounced to me that they had never heard of a propeller being lost. I was feeling down and texted Kande. What she wrote back helped me bounce back. Our family home was 350 kilometers from the marina where Wahine was moored. Sadly, Kande was not able to join often, but I kept her informed of all developments

"Breakdowns can become breakthroughs if you use them right."

Ultimately, I ended up with a three-blade prop, which was a good upgrade on the previous two-blader. It would not give me more speed but would give me more 'bite' in heavy seas, which is always welcome.

Ironically, this was not the first time I had given considerable time, emotional stress and intellectual effort to
the subject of props. Quite a few years ago, I wrote a book
called *Boys Becoming Men*, and in it I explored the absence
of puberty rites of passage (PROPs) for young men in Western society.[3] I referred to the acronym 'PROP' and used the
word 'prop' as a metaphor, pointing out that English has
three meanings for this word.

First, the word 'prop' is used in the world of theatre,
where it means an "ordinary object that is transformed into
something magical that creates the world of fantasy."[4] In
this sense, a prop is temporary and disposable.

In the second usage, the word is both a noun and a verb,
as in 'to prop something up.' It implies stability. If the prop
wasn't present, there would be instability and the danger
of collapse.

The third meaning brings us to the world of transportation, as 'prop' is a shortened version of 'propeller.' Here
is verbatim what I wrote: "A propeller, of course, propels a
craft forward. Without a prop, a boat will drift, and an aircraft will drop. Therefore, a prop is essential for a safe and
successful journey."[5]

These images and usages of the word 'prop' – something
ordinary becoming magical, a buoyancy aid and a device
that provides speed and direction – are relevant to me now.

What now?

I was stuck in *Wahine*'s berth at the Yumenoshima
Marina for two months, unable to get out to sea. I was frus-
trated because I was not doing what I intended – learning
to sail *Wahine* – but it did give me lots to think about. It
felt as if *Wahine* and I were going through a rite of passage
together – and learning to trust each other.

So, with *Wahine* immobile for the foreseeable future, I
tried to make the most of the situation by studying for my

Class 2 Licence, which would allow me to go beyond five miles from land. I also did typhoon training, which covered not only prepping the boat but also remaining on the boat for the typhoon itself. So, I was learning loads.

Once the propeller was installed, it was time for another significant upgrade: the installation of the Hydrovane (a self-steering system that is fuelled by the wind, not by electricity). Being inexperienced in all things mechanical, once again I relied on the help of friends who had joined my shore team: Claude, Rick and the excellent Bobby who managed the installation despite the challenge of fitting into small places to attach the steel plates to the inside of the boat. Hydrovane's strapline is 'Steering the Dream.' While it as tricky to install, the Hydrovane was a dream to operate. When I took *Wahine* out for her first sail with the Hydrovane, I was delighted with how easy it was to set it up and operate. Sailors refer to their Hydrovane as a crew member and often give it a name. In my case, I named her Skylie II, after my border collie, who had accompanied me on some of my bicycle adventures.

Every time I went sailing, I was delighted to have Skylie II as my companion. Over the next few months, I sailed often (sometimes with friends and family accompanying me) and went on two ten-day cruises. Then, at one point in the summer, I decided to try to leave for Canada the following year, a full three years ahead of schedule.

Why?

Times and circumstances had changed. Given so many changing realities, it made sense to leave earlier. At the very least, it would give me a focus to prepare the boat and myself for the solo crossing.

The crossing would see me leaving Tokyo Bay in the late spring of 2021. I would catch the Kuroshio current up the coast of Japan. Then, somewhere off Miyagi or Ibaraki, I would turn *Wahine*'s bow eastward towards my homeland of Canada. The advised route is to sail between latitudes 35N and 40N to my Nemo North.

This would allow me to catch the prevailing winds before turning north at around 149°E avoiding the Pacific High, otherwise known as the windless doldrums, and heading to Vancouver. This route would take me through the two gyres that form the Great Pacific Garbage Patch, which I wanted to witness first-hand so I could share what I saw.

AMAMI OSHIMA SOLO AND ONWARD TO OKINAWA

The plan was to leave Tokyo on a test sail to Amami Oshima (an island between Kyushu Mainland and Okinawa), where I had an invitation from a remote community to visit. I would then go on to Okinawa. The trip from Amami Oshima to Okinawa would take a week non-stop offshore. I'd then harbour-hop back to Tokyo Bay. I would be at sea for about two months, which would be a test of *Wahine*'s and my readiness to do the Pacific crossing. It would be a massive challenge and it sometimes kept me awake at night, dreaming, fretting and planning. In comparison to the North Pacific sail, which loomed large, the Okinawa voyage could have seemed a mere waypoint. But this did not make it any less daunting. Fear is fear, and when you are scared, you are afraid. I was scared! Therefore, I gave the Okinawa trip the respect and attention it deserved.

To get a special certification that would allow my boat to go beyond 40 km offshore, I had to have a particular life raft. It was expensive, of course. At first, the company sent the wrong one. The raft itself was OK, but what was contained within it only met the criteria for going up to 40 km offshore. So, I had to return it two weeks before the departure date to be repacked. It doubled the cost, from $4,000 to $8,000. Gulp. Another reminder that my dream was not only audacious but also expensive.

I had fun while I was waiting for the new raft to arrive. I practised an emergency evacuation of the boat with the old one. It was now over 20 years old and no longer legal. So, with friends gathered around on a cold February day, I threw the life raft overboard to see what would happen. It only half-inflated on the first try because I did not throw it hard enough to pull on the tether cord entirely. The second time I tried, it inflated fully. Wearing a Mustang Survival jacket given to me by David, I leaped into the life raft, now floating firm and erect, to discover what survival provisions were stored inside.

Finally, on 3 March 2021, the life raft arrived and I was ready to go. I ended up leaving Yumenoshima Marina on 4 March, four days later than planned.

A few friends came to see me off. It was a fine, sunny morning when I left the dock for the last time, escorted out into open water by friends in other boats. Before I left the dock, my son Ryan jumped on deck and hugged me goodbye. This was one of many moments of emotion.

Ryan was the chair of my shore team, which was made up of about 20 friends and specialists who knew either me or *Wahine* well – engineers, sailors, mariners, mechanics, electricians and navigators. They all agreed to be on a message string so that if I needed help, they were just a call away. Ryan, who had obtained his own boat operator's licence and, during the Covid-19 pandemic, had stayed on the boat with me for a few weeks, agreed to lead the team.

My project's name was Pacific Solo; however, as a novice sailor, I need the help of others to realize my dream. I was solo on the boat, but I had my team around me.

And so, I left.

I sailed past Tokyo Disneyland, Haneda Airport, Yoko-hama and Yokosuka. Seven hours later, I arrived at Misaki Port. In Misaki, a member of my shore team, Stephan, joined me for a few days to finish the installation of the chart plotter and train me in how to use it and the radar. I would wait a few days to finish these installations and then, when the right weather window arrived, I would sail to Oshima, where Tokyo Bay ends and the Pacific begins. After that, I would stop in Amami Oshima and then on to Okinawa. I was about to learn many more things, not least that Japan has scores of islands who are name OSHIMA!

It was in Misaki that I met Takahashi san. I had heard of him from my friend Bobby, the engineer who had helped me install Skylie II, the Hydrovane. I was surprised and touched that this veteran sailor and boat designer had come and sought me out. He proudly showed me the hulls of his catamaran. I was in awe and remained so. This was the first of many encounters with experienced sailors who have taken the time to befriend me and share their experiences and tips.

Finally, on 9 March, I left Misaki for Oshima after updating my shore team, who were tracking me closely.

This was the beginning of my full-time life on the sea. At that point, when I checked the weather, I observed three things: wind strength and direction, temperature, and the possibility of rain. I have since learned that there are so many more factors I need to consider. For example, the critical information includes not just wind speed but potential gusts, wave height and periods, tidal currents, and CAPE (possibility of lightning and thunder).[6]

But those lessons would come later. For now, it seemed the wind was coming from the northeast, so I would sail the 60 km to Havu Harbour on Oshima, where I had moored before. I knew it would rain, but the wind seemed about right. Little did I know how much I would learn that day and every subsequent day. My learning curve was becoming like a hockey stick – I was not just learning about sailing and the boat itself but also about life at sea and how I needed to learn to live with uncertainty.

Once I cleared the harbour entrance at Misaki, I put up the mainsail and unfurled the foresail. I hand-steered until the sun rose and then I let Skylie II take over.

Despite the rising sun, the skies were grey and there was rain. I cannot recall the wind speed, but *Wahine* was doing well for an hour or so and then suddenly, a gust turned the boat into the wind and I became overpowered. I realized then that I needed to prepare my mainsail to be reefed (reduced in size) adequately. It could have three reefs, but I only had two operating, and the vital one, the third reef, needed in higher winds, needed to be fixed. I had to drop the sail and use the foresail only. Once Oshima appeared through the dismal grey filter and in rising seas and heavier swells, I turned the engine on to stay in control. Entering Havu Harbour was tricky. There were strengthening winds and breaking waves, which, at times, I had to surf to avoid taking big waves on the beam.

I eventually made it into the safe harbour. Once *Wahine* was tied up, I collapsed on the bed, tired and worried about the passage ahead.

I slept for nearly three hours, made a cup of noodles and then took a video call from a filmmaker, Will, who was producing a short film about my quest. I was in a dark place. The seven-hour passage from Misaki had exhausted me, and I was becoming aware of two deficiencies on the boat.

First, I could not put in a third reef, and my autohelm was not working. I had thought I would not need it because I had Skylie II. But I was wrong. The Hydrovane was OK if I was sailing only, but I had to be at the helm when motor sailing.

But the day had brightened. The winds were lessening, the sea became less turbulent and I set out for Okinawa late in the morning, expecting to be at sea for about a week for the next leg of the journey. I left the harbour, sailed into the Pacific and passed several islands in the Izu chain. The sky was blue, and I had a following wind and seas. I was finally out of Tokyo Bay and experiencing the Pacific. I loved how *Wahine* would be lifted by two-metre swells and gently be carried forward – one moment the horizon would be below the boat, and a few seconds later it would be above.

I was about four hours out of Oshima when, through the weak signal left on my phone, the shore crew alerted me to a problem. The tracker that allowed them to watch me was malfunctioning and had me showing up on the rocks around Oshima. They wanted to make sure I was alright. I confirmed that I was, but they asked me to pull in to Niijima to repair the tracker so that the shore team had accurate data on *Wahine's* coordinates and could be sure I was safe. So, I happily pulled into Niijima and began sorting out the problem.

I was still inexperienced at mooring in fishing ports. Captain Hiro, on my shore team, phoned his contacts in the Niijima fishing association, and they told him I was welcome and could dock wherever I wanted. It turns out the dock I moored against was not the best as there were large cavities in the wall, and at that point I was not equipped with 'fender boards' to compensate. Also, the wind was quite gusty, blowing the boat away from the dock, which I naively assumed would be good so my ship would not be slammed against the wall.

I was wrong and nearly lost *Wahine*. When I pulled alongside the pier, the tide was low, which meant I had to leap up on the dock with mooring lines from the boat. With both a bow line and a steer line in hand, I jumped up on the port, expecting to reel the vessel in and tie her up quickly. But with the gusts of wind, *Wahine* lurched away from the dock, nearly pulling me into the sea. I hung on for dear life with the wind forcing *Wahine* away from me and the lines slipping through my hands. I wrapped them around my wrist and, with my butt on the ground and heels digging into the abrasive cement, I used every ounce of strength to manoeuvre my way over to a bollard to tie the bow line. Once that was secure, I got up and dashed to a bollard at the stern to tie up that line. *Wahine* was about five metres from the dock, and the lines were taut! Then slowly, using the friction of the lines around the bollard, I inched her in. An hour later, I had her securely moored, and I collapsed exhausted once again, but this time under blue skies.

It took a little while to discover the problem with the tracker, but in the end it was an easy fix. I had the antenna at an odd angle, which meant the tracker was sending out the wrong data about where I was.

I constantly thought about my voyage and what I had learned. Without autohelm, five to seven days at sea to Okinawa did not seem to be feasible, particularly given that I was not an experienced sailor, so I decided to break the trip up a little and chose my next port in Mie, about 250 km away. It would still test my endurance and skills, but it was doable.

I was posting regularly on the Pacific Solo YouTube channel I had started the previous year, as I was trying to chronicle my progress and my ups and downs. Ryan I had helped me to get it going but now I was largely doing it on my own. In my vlog entry from Havu, I had spoken of how

I needed to navigate my relationship with fear and the difference between fear and terror. Terror can be debilitating as it can freeze us into nonaction or, even worse, the wrong action. On the other hand, fear is a constant companion and we need to form a relationship with it. By being in touch with my fear, I was able to understand that I could be overcome with terror if I attempted to go non-stop to Okinawa, whereas a 250 km passage was doable. The 250 km would take about 30 hours. I knew my capacity for endurance, and I knew that if I broke the 30 hours into increments of six hours, I would succeed.

When I set out at noon on 11 March, I had mapped out my voyage in increments of time:

- Part one: six hours to sunset.
- Part two: six hours to midnight.
- Part three: six hours to sunrise.
- Part four: six hours to land.

The final few hours would be spent following the coast to the safe harbour.

I knew I could do it.

Because of the gusts and where I had chosen to moor, it was challenging to leave the dock. But I finally got *Wahine* free. Once we were clear of the harbour, I hoisted the sails and once again, with a following wind and waves, we pointed our nose towards Mie Prefecture. Blue sky, following seas, fair winds and 250 km to go. I was at peace and happy.

The following 27 hours resulted in not only a change of plans but also a change in me.

The land was out of sight and I only had my compass bearing and electronic chart to guide me. I was watching the weather patterns and I knew that I needed to arrive in the harbour within the 30 hours before conditions changed. Big lesson: the most precise weather prediction is the one you make in the present. I managed a couple of hours of sleep in the early evening, but I was on full alert from then on. I spent the night watching lights and trying to determine the sizes and directions of the various vessels I saw. Were they freighters or fishing fleets? One was likely moving, and the other possibility stationary; freighters would not be at anchor this far out. They were on their way into a port or had left port and were heading into the Pacific. Another light remained inexplicable: it looked like an orb that went lateral quickly, then sped vertically, then came back down to sea level. Then it tracked me for an hour, always at the same bearing. Then it suddenly disappeared.

One big ship tagged me with a laser. I sailed with my navigation lights on and a deck light, which cast a glow on the sails, lighting me up in the darkness and making me more visible. This compensated for my lack of a system called AIS (automatic identification system), which allows boats to identify each other and see what speed and direction they are travelling at. I had an AIS receiver but not a transmitter. So I could spot other vessels on my screen, but they could not spot me.

The following morning I sailed through two storms. The sea often changed from a silky lake-like surface to violent, unpredictable breaking waves. I was at the helm, constantly trying to stay on course. I had foul-weather gear, including high rubber boots. The spray was constant and the occasional wave came into the cockpit. I was grateful for the rainwater, which washed the salt off.

I could not take a break from the helm but discovered that I could pee standing there. I also found myself taking involuntary 30-second naps. With 28 km to go, I wondered what else the passage would throw my way. I soon discovered three- to four-metre waves breaking on my beam. I had to alter course to avoid a knockdown, despite the fact that being closer to land meant I had to deal with the fishing areas marked on the charts.

Being new to navigating, fearful of going down below to check the chart plotter in the heavy seas because of the lack of autohelm and with the battery running low on my phone (which had a backup navigation app), I had to guess the location of the entrance to the inlet containing Shima Yacht Harbour (in Mie). It turned out to be 10 km further than I thought. That was a letdown. Having felt momentary relief in the belief that I would soon be in safe harbour, I had to turn back out into the stormy seas. Once again, I experienced a near knockdown as a rogue wave coincided with a gust, making the boat heel at nearly 70 degrees. A total knockdown would be 90 degrees, with the top of the mast tapping the water. After 4 km, I could turn the boat so that the waves were coming from behind and I could surf the waves the final few hundred metres to the inlet entrance. Finally, the sea calmed as I entered the protected bay and eventually came into the narrow cove of Shima Yacht Harbour.

This time my exhaustion was extreme, but I felt safe. Sleep came easy and lasted several hours.

I woke recalling my 27-hour passage. It seemed surreal as I remembered images that remain imprinted in my mind today. At times it had felt otherworldly. I knew that *Wahine* and I were not ready to cross the Pacific. There were things the boat needed and things for me to learn. I decided to go back to my original plan, to cross before I am 70. In the meantime, I will continue to sail around Japan, exploring its coastline and coastal communities.

EPILOGUE:
THE STORM THAT SWEPT ME TO A MAGICAL PLACE

Part of me was disappointed, of course. However, a friend an advisor, Kirk (who had crossed the Pacific solo from Canada to Japan after four years of sailing the west coast of Canada), made me see reason. He said, "You have zero solo offshore experience – the risk is too significant. It's your life, so do what you like, but you need to train more."

He was right. I decided to slow things down and cruise the Japanese coast for two or three years, gaining experience, learning about the boat and me, and living the dream. I reminded myself that the Pacific Solo project was just a goal and not the essence of my dream. Yes, I dreamed of sailing across an ocean, but fundamentally I dreamed of owning a sailboat, living on her and cruising full time. So, I was already living the dream.

Now I had to inform others. First I consulted with my wife, sons and brother. Then announced my decision to my shore team and then contacted my sponsors. Without exception, everyone was relieved.

I also decided that while I would mostly sail solo, I would sometimes invite crew to sail with me for safety or my training.

To do this I would need to be recertified by the JCI (Japan Craft Inspection Organization), and I wanted to get this done immediately so I could leave Mie with crew. It was in Mie that I met a local strawberry farmer, Katsuya Honda, (who prefers to be called Kaz) who was also a sailor. He was of enormous help to me in a number of ways, not least driving me to the JCI office, where I applied for my new certificate for *Wahine*. Kaz was new to the JCI registration process, but I was helped greatly with this and on other occasions by Captain Hiro, a shore team member who was always willing to get on the phone to speak with JCI as well as other authorities (such as the Coast Guard) when I needed support and help. The only problem is that to get a permanent certificate , I had to take the boat out of the water and be inspected on land. Unfortunately, there was no place available willing to take me due to the lock down. So, I was able to get a 30 day temporary permit that allowed me to sail distant from land and have up to five crew members.

From Mie I sailed with two shore team members, the aforementioned Stephan and also Gregor around Kii Hanto to the port town of Tanabe in Wakayama Prefecture. From there I sailed solo to Shikoku, stopping at several ports along the way. I eventually arrived at Oita, where I was told I could haul my boat out for a hull inspection in order to get the new permanent certification. I had wanted to do this in Mie or Osaka; however, because of the pandemic, I had not been allowed to enter any of the ports where I could bring *Wahine* on land.

In the meantime, the History Channel had asked if they could shoot a pilot for a potential series called *Dare to Dream*, which would feature "an old guy (me) learning a new hobby (sailing) and experiencing remote Japan from the sea." I agreed and, after much discussion, we decided that the first location would be Amami Oshima. I had been invited to visit this remote community by a friend of a friend. Matt worked for the mayor of one of the communities to promote tourism. He is an Australian who had worked for a large PR firm in Tokyo and he leaped at the chance to live on this unique island where some people still hunted wild boar and caught deadly snakes for a living. Matt helped the History Channel crew to set up an itinerary and watched for my weather window to sail down.

One of my patrons and shore team, Robin,who had become a trusted friend, supporter, and a sailor himself, joined me on a passage planned to last two or three days. I was now in Miyazaki, a beautiful stretch of coastline in Kyushu with abundant palm trees and surfers. Initially I docked in Miyazaki Marina, which has a narrow and hazardous entrance due to sediment that gathers, causing the channel to become shallow and need dredging. However, I met a boat broker, Hara Atsushi, who invited me to moor for free in his hometown of Abaratsu so I went a further 60 km south and pulled into the big, deep harbour. Having learned my lesson at Niijima, where I had been slammed against and then away from a wall, chafing several lines to ruination and almost losing my boat, I knew it was always better to tie to a floating pontoon that rose and fell with the tide than a hard wall as is usual in fishing ports. Hara-san had told me the harbour had a wall but that there was an abandoned fishing vessel I could tie up to, with the vessel acting as a pontoon.

So, I arrived and did exactly that. The abandoned ship was old and had been the site of many drinking parties. So, after tying up, I grabbed a couple of garbage bags and cleaned the boat to make a more pleasant route as I crossed over from my ship to land.

Around this time something scary was happening at sea. A few months earlier, in August 2021, a new island had formed off the course of Japan, a few hundred miles from Tokyo. An underwater volcano had erupted, creating the islet and releasing a floating island of pumice, or what the Japanese call *karuishi* (small rock).

I was advised not to come to Amami Oshima as the harbours were plugged with pumice. Once again, the silver lining was that as I researched how this *karuishi* could affect a boat, I learned more about seawater's role in keeping a diesel engine cool. Critically, the motor could be severely damaged if the seawater intake valve also took in the pumice. Going to Amami Oshima, the island with Jurassic-like beaches, would have to wait. The History Channel and I looked for alternatives. We found one: an island in the Nagasaki Goto archipelago, to the north.

By this time, Kirk Patterson, known for his remarkable solo Pacific crossing and being the first foreigner to circumnavigate Japan, became an advisor for the History Channel series. Under his recommendation, we set our sights on Nagasaki's Goto Islands. I arrived a few days before the History Channel crew. However, the emergence of the Omicron covid variant led to the cancellation of filming by the island's mayor. Thanks to Kirk's resourcefulness, we swiftly shifted our focus to Ikijima, where we successfully filmed the pilot in April 2021. My voyage there had its share of challenges, including a coast guard rescue, a tow, and a significant repair, with Kirk Patterson playing a pivotal role in orchestrating my rescue and resolving the repair issues. The week of filming with Yuji and his crew and assisted by Harbour Master Masutaka Hayashida, was nothing short of spectacular and well worth all the effort and hassle.

Amid all this, I needed to continue finding a way to fund my dream. I was enjoying moderate success in recruiting sponsors, and another sailor was referred to me as a 'sponsorship ninja.' He described me as a 'tiny YouTube channel' (he was right, as I still had fewer than 1,000 subscribers), but saw that I'd had significant success with cash sponsors.

But I had to do better in creating a steady income. I was no longer salaried, and my only regular income came from two government pensions amounting to about $500 a month. I had already cashed in a small private pension to help purchase the *Wahine*, and my initial sponsorship money had gone to complete the purchase, upgrade equipment on the boat running costs.

But I had to do more. I had wanted to return to speaking, writing and consulting with Navigate22. I had made some money in 2020, but I needed more. But also, I needed to be sailing full time to gain experienced. In the meantime, I had noticed an increasing number of people following me because, like me, they considered themselves to be what came to be called 'Never-Too-Laters.' They too were inspired to find ways to fulfil their dreams no matter their age, and often they asked me for advice on how to do this.

This was the birth of the Never Too Late Academy, which I formed initially with my long-time friend Mark McBennett. Soon after we were joined by a group of investors, also long-time friends.

I was becoming a digital nomad – turning a hobby into a business and doing it all from *Wahine*. I was living the dream. Pacific Solo was the goal that helped me strive towards the vision. The thought buoyed me that I was one of the New Rich, a term coined by Timothy Ferriss in *The 4-Hour Work-week*.[7] I was rich in time, mobility and relationships.

POSTSCRIPT

In March 2023 shortly before submitting the manuscript for this book to the publisher, I finally arrived in Amami Oshima and was welcomed by the mayor of Uken Son and Matt, who had initially invited me to visit the remote harbour. It was my third attempt in two years. And even this attempt had its challenges.

Having circumnavigated Kyushu in the spring of 2022, I spent a few months exploring parts of the Seto Inland Sea, where I got to know Daniel Springett, an experienced sailor, and fellow YouTuber. Two shore team members, Anthony and Nikola joined me from Tokyo an hour before a late afternoon departure. We bid farewell to Daniel, knowing we had a long cold night ahead navigating currents, islands, and busy shipping routes with the aim of navigating the narrow straits between NW Shikoku and Kyushu at slack tide, only to be forced to stop in Oita due to freezing temperatures and electrical problems. I then set out again in February 2023 to sail non-stop, but was forced after 30 hours to pull in to Abaratsu because of a failing alternator this time with my colleague from the Never Too Late Academy, Esteban. After a week there, I set sail with the bow pointed to Amami Oshima expecting to make one stop along the way. It would take two to three days. Shintaro Hirayama, who I had known for a couple of years, asked if he could join me. I am glad I said yes as he was of great help during one of my scariest 24 hours at sea. First stop though was Tanegashima, the Cape the Cape Canaveral of Japan, where we spent a delightful two days.

Then I embarked on a non-stop about 300 kilometers to Amami Oshima only to find myself adrift in the middle of a very dark night with little wind or engine and having to dodge ships coming in both directions with only the incandescent glow of a nearby volcano and the welcoming beam of a lighthouse to assist me. Finally, in the morning with a slight change in the wind, I decided to sail to the lighthouse, which was about 40 kms away, only for the wind to change half way there and come from the opposite direction in force.

With building seas, four-metre waves and 30-knot winds, I was being blown towards the volcano. However, with the help of Shin Taro (my crew member), the shore team and Elon Musk's Starlink, I was able to get the engine going and motor into the tiny harbour on the remote island of Akuse-kishima. Only 59 people live there, but the three days I spent there made the storm and the engine problems worth it. If not for those adversities, I would not have discovered this divine island.

Finally the storm subsided and we decided to stay on Akuseki Jima for three days to explore and repair some of the damage from the storm. Then under blue skies and calm seas, we set sail finally arriving Amami two years after I first left Tokyo with Amami as the destination and the third attempt. I kissed the ground and finally met Matt and the Mayor for the first time. I felt like I had come home

In the following pages, I will share with you what I have learned about dreams, how to recognize and realize them, and how to embrace the joy that comes from achieving them.

PART TWO

DARE:

A FOUR-STEP PROGRAMME TO REDESIGN YOUR LIFE

The title of this book is *Dare to Dream*. Before I take you through a four-step programme to realize your audacious dream, let's consider the verb 'to dare.'

While much of what I lay out in this book can be applied to goal-setting generally, I am primarily concerned with high-stakes dreams. A high-stakes dream is something beyond an ordinary life milestone, such as graduating, finding a job, finding a partner, buying a house or moving to a new place. The audacious kind of dream I'm talking about is one with significant risk, where you just know that it is something you want to realize before you die. It is not simply a bucket list item; instead, you believe that you will die with great regret if it does not happen.

It is something that you will dare to try. The use of the word 'dare' implies there is risk and therefore fear. There is a risk and, indeed, the possibility of failure. The stakes are high. But also, the rewards are high because the dream that you harbour will be significant for you and will also affect others. It will become part of your legacy. The adage 'nothing ventured, nothing gained' is true. I want to help you identify that dream, that aspiration, that vision, and find the courage and tools you need to see it become a reality. So, let's go. First, we need to detect what dream is powerful enough to pull you from your comfort zone to reach new heights.

Often these dreams and goals are born at our darkest moments. When we have encountered failure, we need to trigger resilience. It is often then that a resolve bubbles from the soul to the surface of our intentions and self-perception.

But before we begin to dig into these possibilities, let me ask you if you feel you are part of the fourth culture, or want to be.

The name 'third-culture kids' refers to children of missionaries who were raised in international schools back in the 1980s. In my view, it was a slightly derogatory term. It was born out of pastoral concern for kids who were living abroad with their parents and who weren't completely at home in their host culture, but neither did they feel part of their home culture. They were not home. They were part of a third culture. Academics studied them and counsellors helped them cope.

However, over time, it became evident that third-culture kids no longer needed this pastoral concern. Instead, they began to be seen – and to see themselves – as global citizens. Third-culture kids were happy in their own skin. I know because I married one. One of the things that attracted me to my wife Kande, who had been raised in an international school, was how comfortable she was crossing borders, how wide her network of friends was around the world and how comfortable she was in her own skin.

The world has moved on. We are now seeing the emergence of a 'fourth culture' – not just kids but adults, families and emerging communities that are global citizens or even digital nomads. They are similar to third-culture kids in that they cross borders effortlessly, but they are different as they are not beholden to corporate careers and rather live alternative lifestyles, living life on their own terms.

Two things have fuelled the rise of the fourth culture. First of all, technology has enabled people to create revenue streams outside of the nine to five. The second factor is the Covid-19 pandemic, where remote working and working at home became necessary and then remained in place in many organizations as many people realized they wanted to live life on their own terms.

Whereas international schools are an index for the rise of the third culture, the index for the fourth culture is probably online commerce. I was curious to know , so I hired a researcher to review YT statistics. She discovered through a deep dive that that ten years ago there were only 800 You-Tube channels that were monetized, whereas today there are two million. Not all of those channel owners are earning a full-time living from their channel but many are, and some are not only millionaires but now billionaires. I have become part of one community within the fourth culture. It is the sailing community, many of whom have their own channels. A few years ago there was just a handful of small YouTube sailing channels, with a few followers. Today there are thousands, with many earning a full-time income from their videos and associated activities.

If you recognize yourself in this description, chances are you're a fourth-culture person.

So, with this context in mind, let's consider the four steps of DARE: a programme to help you redesign your life.

STEP 1:
DETECT

It surprises me how many people cannot identify their dreams. They have set goals for their career, family and education. They may even have created a bucket list of things they look forward to doing or seeing someday. But when it comes to a compelling dream that they would regret not realizing, they have nothing.

Yet many people feel a yearning – a longing for meaning, purpose and a sense of higher calling. A feeling that there is something more beyond the horizon. If this idea resonates with you, read on carefully and embrace what I am about to say. It could change your life.

I am not talking about the mere search for meaning but, in the words of the American writer Joseph Campbell, about "the experience of life."[8] I have found that the older I get, the more I turn to my inner life. I want to see myself through the filter of the universe, not the universe through my filter.

Let's apply a detection device to your life and see what we can discover. Some finds may be exciting but not precious.

We are looking for what is precious – gold, not copper. We may find it in the roughest parts of your life. Dreams are crushed by the pressures of living, such as responsibilities, defeats, failures and obligations. But we realize our dreams because of those pressures; charcoal can become a diamond. That is what we are searching for.

Let's return to your childhood – things you dreamed about during the day, that took your breath away as you imagined yourself. Visions of you in the future. Here we will find the seeds of that one thing or one of many that brings a tingle of fear because it seems daring. And, crucially, when you are being honest with yourself, you know you want to at least try it before you die.

Metal detectors transmit electromagnetic energy into the ground. Any metal objects within range will be energized to retransmit to an electromagnetic field. The frequency of the metal detector determines the size and depth of the objects it can find. Lower frequencies will detect larger and deeper objects, and higher frequencies will detect smaller and shallower objects. The ground balance setting matters for the type of soil and how much other noise there is. Also, the discrimination setting matters so that you can correctly identify what kind of object you have found.

Our Dream Detector does much the same thing. We are looking for something precious that has been buried deep and forgotten.

Dreams fascinate us and occupy our thoughts and fantasies. A dream worth pursuing grabs your attention and brings a focus on a higher purpose. It gets you out of bed in the morning. Also, a dream worth pursuing leaves a legacy.

Dreams can be our waking fantasies – daydreams – but they can also be what fills our imagination while we are asleep. Both can fuel or diminish our sense of purpose and affect our motivation. Night dreaming draws on our subconscious, which can be seeded by our daydreams.

Daydreams can be formative for children – they were for me. Children need to be allowed to dream. Gail Saltz, a psychiatrist and author of *The Power of Different*, says of daydreams, "They are a way of being creative, problem-solving, and comforting oneself. It is essential to let your mind wander."[9] While a daydreaming session can provide an escape, it is nonetheless deliberative and reveals who you are and what you desire to be.

In my life, I have had lots of dreams and goals. These are things I think about during the day, and they often fuel my dreams in some way or another at night. My list so far:

- Age 10: Having a life of adventure, endurance and purpose. This was a dream I woke up from in the middle of the night. It was my first epiphany.
- Age 12: Having a bedroom of my own.
- Age 13: Living on a sailboat, writing books and learning to fly.
- Age 14: Fitting in.
- Age 15: Figuring out who I was.

SIFTING YOUR DREAMS

"Please tell me how you evaluate the right dream from the wrong dream?"

The man asking this question was two years from retirement. He was a senior executive of a manufacturing company, and we had met in a port town where my boat and I were berthed for a few weeks.

We had many conversations about dreams and what it means to be a Never-Too-Later. Shortly after I sailed to another port, the man sent me this question. I knew he was searching for something meaningful to focus on in retirement. I sensed he was both elated at the prospect of retiring and, at the same time, unsettled. His childhood dreams and fantasies were buried under tons of adult responsibility.

My response was to ask him, "What matters more to you than anything else? If you are to achieve one thing before you die, what will it be? You have to reach beyond good ideas and curiosities and search your soul and psyche for those ambitious dreams that will transform your life and positively affect others too! Once you identify those dreams, you can begin to consider possible road maps – or goals – to enable you to realize them."

Another man I spoke with, in his late fifties, was already realizing an audacious dream. We talked about the idea of 'goals to the power of two': dreams that are exponentially powerful, transformative and not only for you but for others as well.

This is 'dream squared,' or D2.

It is the anatomy of this kind of dream that intrigues me. How do you find this kind of exponential dream: a highly infectious dream that pulls in others and will leave a legacy?

Here are the characteristics of a dream worth pursuing:

- It leaves a legacy.
- It involves others.
- It transforms you.

So, we are looking for something more profound and personal than a daydream or a nightdream. Your dream life will be affected by it, for sure, but the dream we want to detect is on a higher plane. It is about discovering your calling and your purpose. You will discover your exponential dream in its effect on your life and others'. It will be something that takes into account your life so far.

I have already referred to the idea of a Dream Detector being akin to a metal detector. A metal detector emits a frequency that reacts with a metal object, causing that object to emit a frequency back. In the same way, when you search for a dream, it will speak to you. It will emit a 'signal' that resonates with you as if your soul was saying something. Often dreams can lie dormant for years and decades. You may have forgotten that they existed – dismissed them as juvenile or allowed them to be crushed by other aspects of your life. But when you enter detection mode and turn on your Dream Detector to search for buried treasure, that dormant dream will come alive again and begin speaking back to you. Then you can start to determine the dream and its qualities.

As I write, I look at what I call our 'landmark tree' in my front yard. But establishing this landmark was not a straightforward process.

In 2005, my wife and I bought a piece of mountainside land – part abandoned garden and part orchard. When we moved in, we planted over 300 trees and bushes. Among these were quite a few trees of different species. One particular tree we planted was the so-called princess tree, known in Japan as a *kiri* tree and outside Japan as a paulownia. I was attracted to it because it is fast-growing and good for the environment.

At maturity, the *kiri* tree absorbs enormous amounts of carbon from the atmosphere. One acre of *kiri* can absorb 90 tonnes of carbon dioxide a year. That is huge, and I liked the idea of cleansing the air around us. But even more attractive to me were the tree's oxygen-producing qualities. The *kiri* has large leaves, which are oxygen-making machines. Then there is the cultural aspect. I learned that *kiri* trees grow quickly and mature (at about 10 metres) after about 20 years. In Japan, a person is considered to be an adult at the age of 20. A *kiri* tree would be planted when a daughter was born. Then, when that daughter came of age, the tree would be cut down and the wood used to make furniture.

So, in my research on which trees to plant, the *kiri* tree was high on the list. We planted four of them, and soon they were well on the way to becoming landmark trees. But it wasn't to be.

We discovered that they were not strong trees in a storm, because the trunk is tubular with a hollow shaft in the middle (unlike in other trees, which are solid all the way through). *Kiri* trees, therefore, do not have the strength to withstand high winds. And, one by one, as the four trees grew, they blew over. My wife was not sad to see them go. Their vast leaves often fell and were difficult to rake up because of their size. They had to be picked up one by one. But it was their lightweight trunk and shallow roots that were their downfall. They fell quickly.

We had, however, planted another tree we had intended to be a landmark tree. It was a Himalayan pine, and we paid nearly $2,000 for it. It was spindly and about six feet tall. Sadly, while it grew slowly, it too did not fare well in high winds. It was knocked over three times by typhoons. Its roots had not gone deep, and with each knockdown they were weakened further. Because of the amount of money we had spent on this tree, I put in considerable effort each time to right it with ropes and guidelines. Then after a few months, I would remove the supporting strings and a typhoon would come, and the tree would fall over again. Finally, I accepted that the tree and our land did not fit. So the next time it blew over, I cut it up for firewood.

The tree I am looking at as I write became our landmark tree by accident. It was given to us by our gardener. He had removed it from another client's garden and felt it would grow well in our soil. He was right. It is now the tallest tree on our property. We love that tree.

A landmark tree has unique characteristics:

1. It is visible, which means it helps to define you and your land. It can be seen from a distance and provide a visual bearing on where *home* is. It's important to know where home is.
2. It gives you a vantage point. When climbed, it offers a great view of the distant horizon and what surrounds you.
3. It is solid and durable.

In the process of sifting through your dreams, you are looking for that kind of dream – a dream that, when spotted, is obvious. Our landmark tree gives me a bearing and offers me a perspective on what is beyond me and where I could go. It inspires me and is exceedingly pleasing to see.

I also note that it differs from the original tree we thought would be our landmark.

Like the Himalayan pine and the *kiri* trees on our property, some dreams come, dominate for a short time but then disappear, failing to stand the test of time. But others can come almost by accident. You might find that, when passing dreams give up their space in your dreamscape, a new dream grows and becomes part of your life. When you take the time to stroll through the garden of your life, you may realize that this tree has become vital to you and offers you a bearing as well as a vantage point.

So, to detect what dreams are important to you, you will need to return to your formative years. What dreams did you plant early on and which dreams have survived, albeit in a dormant state? Which dreams give you a perspective on the future and a reminder of home? Here is where you will find something of value.

Going back to the metaphor of detecting metal, just as there are a variety of metal, dreams vary in size, depth and essential mineral qualities. The frequency of a metal detector determines the size and depth of the objects it can find. Lower frequencies will detect larger and deeper objects, and higher frequencies will detect smaller and shallower objects. And the discrimination setting matters so that you can correctly identify what kind of object you have found.

Similarly, your Dream Detector needs to be able to find dreams at all depths, of all sizes and of all types of mineral. As we scan our childhood dreams and aspirations, we will find all kinds of plans and impulses. But we are looking for dreams that continue to fascinate and inspire us. Particularly, we should look back at times of crisis or challenge, when we felt we were being crushed, for it is there that we will often find the nugget of hope that draws us forward.

As we discover nuggets, we should examine them carefully. In the next step, we will seek to amplify those nuggets, and we will do that by defining ourselves and our mission in life.

STEP 2: AMPLIFY

A dream becomes your horizon, and you develop a sense of mission about getting there. It's your bearing. Goals are the incremental steps necessary to realize your dream and fulfil your mission, and one way of translating your dream into tangible dreams is to write a mission statement.

When people think of a mission statement, they often think of something to put in their résumé, CV or LinkedIn profile. In other words, they craft something they hope will shape others' perceptions of them. But the first step is to find out who you are and where you want to go. Writing a mission statement that you can read to the person in the mirror is better. It says, "This is who I am and where I want to go." It may form the basis for a public version, but ultimately it is something you own, believe in and aspire to.

At this point we are still in detection mode but coming closer to identifying your dream. We will use a personal mission statement to do this. But, before we do, we need to take a step back and look at a 360-degree view of your life – past, present and future.

Why? This story will help you understand. It illustrates the importance of understanding the past and having a vision of the future.

It's about tsunami stones, which I first learned about just after the triple disaster that struck Japan in 2011, when Sato-san, an elder on the island of Miyato-jima, told me this story. We were sitting on the gymnasium floor of the school he had attended decades ago. A couple of hundred others were also on the floor. Some were sleeping; some were eating; some were just sitting in silence. It was days after the tsunami, which had swept away their houses, but no lives had been lost on this particular island. Sato-san told me of the last time a tsunami had swept over their island, more than 1,200 years earlier. Modern-day geologists say there was a magnitude 9.0 earthquake in the sea not too far away. The villagers had been taught to move to higher ground when the earth shook. So, they did; half of the village went to a nearby hill, and the others went to a higher elevation slightly further away. From their vantage points, they witnessed the incoming wave. They saw the waters of Ishinomaki Bay rise and, as the giant swell entered the expansive harbour, the tide grew in height and speed. They watched in horror as their houses and fishing boats were destroyed below them.

The folks on the higher hill had a 360-degree view of the island, in contrast to the limited view of those on the lower elevation. From their vantage point, they could see something that those on the lower hill could not: a second wave, which had circled the island, was now rushing up the valley of rice paddies and it collided with the first wave in the village below. The waters rose violently upwards, enveloping the first hill and sweeping off everyone and everything on it.

The horrified survivors rebuilt their homes and fishing boats and carved and erected tsunami stones on the first hill. This was in part to mourn the ones they had lost but also to warn future generations that if they felt the earth shake, they should not come to that hill but should instead go to the higher one.

I discovered later that there are hundreds of such warning stones along the coast of Japan, marking where previous tsunamis have come onshore.

For 50 generations, children were taken to the top of that hill on Miyato-jima to read the stone and be told to heed the message.

Sato-san, now in his seventies, told me that it was part of the curriculum of the local elementary school – the one where the survivors were now taking refuge in 2011. He said he had been seven years old when his class had been led to the top of the hill to read the words and hear what had happened.

So, on 11 March 2011, in mid-afternoon, the whole community knew what to do when the earth shook. They went to the top of the further, higher hill and waited and watched. But they did not need to wait long. Just a few minutes after their arrival, they saw the waters rise and rush into the harbour, destroying their homes and boats. And then, for the first time in 1,200 years, people on that hill watched as the second wave came in, colliding with the first and rising violently until the first hill disappeared and washed that stone away. Sato-san said with a slight smile that this time no one had lost their lives, thanks to the foresight of their predecessors over a millennium ago.

I stress again that finding your dream is about more than writing an idea down on a bucket list. Yes, it is something deeply personal, something you look forward to, but it must also be something that will impact your world now and in the future. Often these dreams come by accident, so we need to look into the crevices of our lives at the lessons we have learned and at what seeds of destiny have been planted.

As that village in Japan experienced over a millennium ago, disasters, setbacks and pivots can result in us going to higher ground for an unobstructed view.

We are trying to detect that sense of wonder, to give us insight into our dream. We want to find a vision of ourselves and our future that takes our breath away and casts a spell on us – that makes it difficult for us to take our eyes off the subject of our awe. It is here where we find what Campbell calls the "experience of life."[10]

EXERCISE 1

- List the parts of your life that you would describe as following a straight line. How could you bring variety and diversity into your life just now?
- Is your social network simply an extension of your tastes and experience? If so, look for opportunities to add to your social repertoire.
- How do you view failure and hard times? Make a list of what good has come to you because of them.
- Review and reevaluate your values and mission. What is the bedrock of your life's mission and values?
- Jot down a story of hope or the name of someone who inspires you and meditate on these things.

This exercise will help you to find clarity about your life's mission. A vision of the future can be a powerful force that pulls you further and higher than you have ever been before.

Navigation requires a bearing, a destination. Sometimes the objective is clearly in view. At other times it is obscured by bad weather, seemingly giant obstacles and enforced detours – yet the goal still mysteriously, inexplicably lures you forward.

Take a fresh look at your life's mission and perhaps allocate a new set of words and points of reference to determine what is luring you forward. What is it in the core of you that makes you want to live and achieve? For me as a youngster I had visions of myself traveling, crossing deserts, writing books, etc. They filled my fantasy time. What fills yours?

Write down the first sentence or two that come to you to describe your 'bearing,' or the goal that draws you forward. If it helps go back to your play time as a child. What were your fantasies. How did you view yourself. What did you imagine.

Remember: this is primarily for you, not for others. You may use it in a CV or bio, but that is not its main purpose. It is for you to articulate clearly to yourself your bearing and trajectory.

To find that place of mission and calling and to be able to articulate it, we need to appreciate the value of words. I lived in the UK for 13 years, and what I most missed when I left was the conversation. I confess I did not miss the weather or the food. But I found that even conversation with children was rich as their vocabulary was extensive and they chose words with precision.

EXERCISE 2

To hone our appreciation of words, let's do an exercise together. Do it right now – it won't take long. It is preparation for writing your mission statement.

The exercise involves choosing three words. Here are the criteria:

- For **Word 1**, choose one that you like to use. I am not talking about a 'filler' word that you use frequently (such as umm, aww, look, awesome, cool, etc). It should be a word that you enjoy including in a sentence because it has precision. It could be a monosyllabic word, such as 'grace,' or a multisyllabic word, such as 'surreptitious.' I use these words as examples because I recall that they interested me when I first encountered them. I pondered them, and they became part of my vocabulary – not used often but used precisely.

- For **Word 2**, think back to one you have heard or read in the past couple of months or even past couple of years. Identify one where, when you first heard it, it helped to shed light on a concept or notion. For me, this happened the first time I heard 'surreptitious.' I paused, I liked it and I enjoyed it. More recently 'proclivity' has become part of my lexicon. I ensure not to overuse new found words but they do enrich my thought life.

- For **Word 3**, search for a brand new word – one that you have never heard or read before. Read a book on a different subject to that which you are accustomed, or look in a dictionary or perhaps a thesaurus. Then choose and own your new word. You are not looking for a word that you think will impress but rather a word that gives you a tingle because of its precision and its power to illuminate. As I write, I did this exercise a fresh. I went on a word adventure and discovered many new ones , but the one that jumped at me, and made me think, and I thought is powerfully precise is 'obliquity': the idea that sometimes we reach our goals indirectly, often by pursuing something else entirely, suggesting that the pursuit of happiness can take unexpected paths.

This exercise will help us in two ways. First, it reminds us of the importance of the words that we use and their precise meaning. Second, the actual words you choose may give you a clue as to where your passions lie.

WRITING YOUR MISSION STATEMENT

Now that you are warmed up, let's move on to writing your mission statement. Look in the mirror and write down what you see and want to see regarding your life goal, your calling and your mission. This is for you – no one else. You are not trying to impress a future employer, your family or your friends. You are simply being true to yourself – both you now and you in the future.

Go ahead and commit to paper – I dare you. You can always change it later. Write it down and then read it out loud to yourself.

STEP 3:
READY

In the midst of writing this book, I visited the Annapolis Boat Show, where I met with fellow YouTubers who had sailing channels. I asked many of them for their number one tip for those considering an audacious dream. Most of them were younger, almost all couples, and they had all chosen an alternative lifestyle.

The number one tip was "just do it." They phrased this advice in different ways – "just go," "go for it," "just throw the lines." But the message was the same: just *go*.

Realizing a dream requires you to take a first step – which requires more than dreaming. It requires you to put pen to paper or finger to keyboard, write out a plan and identify milestones to achieve your dream. At some point, when you have gone beyond the point of no return, you need to pull the trigger – that's the 'just go' part. But to get there, you must get ready. And getting ready means you need metrics to measure your progress.

We live in an age of analytics. Unless you are a hermit and have no social media at all, you have access to data and metrics about your online presence and habits, and those of the people you are linked to.

In my preparations to leave the Port of Tokyo for what I thought would be the last time in February 2021, I set myself readiness goals. My aim was to be at least 80% ready for the stress test sail to Okinawa and 100% ready for my eventual crossing of the Pacific.

I established four tracks of readiness:

- **Wahine:** *Wahine* needed several things to be upgraded, added or repaired before she could receive the certification required to be allowed to go off-shore. These included a new jib sail, furler, storm sail and life raft; a suite of electronics; plus, ideally, solar and hydro generators.
- **Me:** I needed to be ready physically and mentally. I spent a lot of time thinking about these readiness goals. UFC Gym Japan acted as my fitness sponsor and its trainers focused on my ability to be agile on the boat. Mentally, I knew I had to be ready to live solo. This was daunting, so I set goals to be on my own more and more and also to read books written by those who had lived a life of solitude at sea and on the land.
- **Financial:** My dream was not a cheap one and I knew that I would have to be successful in generating cash and carefully managing it.
- **Education:** I also had goals in terms of informing and inspiring others about what it means to have an adventure with purpose, and bringing attention to the world's oceans.

I had much to do.

While many of the goals were practical and measurable, the mental fitness aspects was less so. So, I pondered a lot about how to prepare for isolation, seclusion, solitude and loneliness. These are things that cause sailors to crack, I am told. From what I have read, I understand that hallucinations, hearing voices and nightmares are common for the solo sailor. To be frank, the prospect of being alone in the middle of the North Pacific was unsettling at best, and at times terrifying.

As a result, I made a note of three tips.

The first was to look to the large, distant horizon and ponder the profound. A boat has many portholes and hatches. I have discovered that each offers a slightly different perspective on the world outside and a view of the horizon. And also, each reminds me that the world out there is larger than my confined space. Each porthole, for me, offers a slightly different horizon and possibilities.

The second was to look to the near and tiny horizon and search for the magical. I relearned how to walk around my small space with the spirit of exploration and adventure. One of my favourite travel books, called *Voyage Around My Room*, was written in 1794 by a Frenchman, Xavier de Maistre. He was confined to his room for six weeks, during which he chronicled his travels around his room. "When I travel through my room, I rarely follow a straight line," he writes.[11]

It is a wonderfully fascinating read as it transforms a small space into a universe to be explored. By the way, de Maistre found so much from his discovery that he wrote a sequel, called *A Nocturnal Expedition Around My Room*, in which he ventured out on his balcony!

The third tip was to look to the inner horizon in search of comedy. Laughter is a great stimulus. It brings a change of attitude. It is, in fact, contagious in spreading joy. I learned a huge amount as I prepared for my voyage, and most of my learning was the result of failure. Sometimes, my mistakes were so stupid I could only laugh at my own expense. Then, there were the moments of pure, joyous laughter when I solved a problem I had thought was insurmountable. Whatever the cause of the laughter, I found it was a contagion that infected my soul and spread throughout my life. Quite simply, laughter is uplifting.

Measuring our readiness, requires us to set goals and move towards them. For a dream to become realized, it must first become our mission, and in turn the mission must be given goals and plans to achieve them. Each goal achieved readies for the realization of our dream.

STEP 4:
ENJOY

This brings me back to the advice given to me by the old sea dog in Misaki, Taro Takahashi. As a refresher, his advice to me was threefold:

1. Don't fall overboard.
2. Stay calm. Panic does not help.
3. When things are tough, remember that this is your dream. You chose to be here. So, be happy!

His advice has stuck with me. But it takes deliberate intent to celebrate and be joyful. Yes, at times, the laughter will come upon you unexpectedly – out of nowhere, you will be struck with joy and laughter. But it is also critical that you plan for it. You must acknowledge milestones and appropriately celebrate even small steps towards your goal. I would go so far as to say you need to ritualize your celebration of key moments.

This means you have to open your heart. It sounds like a cliché, but I know no other way to say it. If the heart is the symbol of the seat of emotion, then to realize our dream and truly appreciate that we have accomplished it (or just taken a step towards it, or perhaps a step away if we realize that is the best course of action), we need to feel the highs and lows of emotion.

As I was readying *Wahine* and myself for departure from the marina at Yumenoshima (which, as you'll recall, means Island of Dreams), I decided to have a day where all of *Wahine*'s former and new crew and friends could come and celebrate her. I deliberately chose Valentine's Day for this event. Long before I became her guardian, she had called Yumenoshima Marina her home. It seemed only fitting that the people who had sailed on her and helped me learn about her and upgrade her should have the opportunity to come and say goodbye.

It was unexpectedly emotional for me. Milestone moments are emotional.

Years ago, while I was in Bosnia, I sought advice from some UN soldiers with whom I had become acquainted about how to cope with suffering. They said you have to turn the volume down on your emotions. Doing this embraces the 'principle of least interest.' Which essentially, to succeed you must not care. Often practised in business and even personal relationships, the principle embraces the notion that whoever has the least interest in the outcome has the greatest power.

While I respect this perspective, and appreciate its wisdom amidst the chaos and violence of war, it is a principle I have chosen *not* to live my life by. Rather, I have made a conscious decision to care and to care deeply, believing that this is what makes us human. I have found that rather than being debilitating, it is empowering.

So, milestone moments – intersections we mark with emotion – allow us to move on.

I have been praised but also sometimes criticized for recruiting sponsors. The criticism has come from others who have funded their own dreams. But, in almost every case, my sponsorships have resulted from deep friendships and a long relationship of trust and mutual support. That makes me all the more grateful, and even emotional, that these friends of mine have stood with me. I also have friends – very good friends – who said that even if I didn't ask for sponsors, they would support me because they were scared for me. I respect their concern because they did not want to feel culpable if my life was put in danger.

Relationships matter to me. Longevity of friendship matters. I have an inner circle of friends, but it is not exclusive. It grows as trust and respect grow. It grieves me deeply when relationships end, whether through death or when the connection breaks down due to an argument or loss of trust. But, even then, my hope is always that redemption and grace will help to restore the relationship

For me, redemption and grace are concepts I live by. Loving, and being loved, are unconditional. But this is not always easy.

But back to *Wahine*'s farewell party...

I felt the emotions of the event more deeply than I had expected. I looked at those who had gathered (scattered across the dock) and thought of others who had not been able to come, and the thought of taking *Wahine* from her decade-long home was significant. So, the tears came. But then I moved on. The light was green, the tears dried, and I celebrated the progress that had been made in preparing for the voyage and the people who joined me in caring.

So, choose to feel! Choose to embrace the moment's emotion and let your soul soar to the heights of what it means to be human.

To enjoy simply means to experience joy. But what is joy?

C. S. Lewis describes it this way:

> Joy (in my sense) has one characteristic indeed, and one only, in common with them; the fact that anyone who has experienced it will want it again... I doubt whether anyone who has tasted it would ever, if both were in his power, exchange it for all the pleasures in the world.[12]

Joy happens in two ways. It can erupt suddenly, but it can also be triggered with intention.

Often in life, we are going about our daily routine in our usual cadence and joy surprises us. This is not necessarily in the profoundly spiritual or intensely intellectual way C. S. Lewis describes. Nonetheless, it is spiritual in texture and is unexpected. It's what I call a Jack-in-the-box experience. You are turning the handle of life, abiding by a certain rhythm and consistency. Then, the box explodes without warning and a clown pops out, changing the routine into a moment of laughter and hilarious distraction. These moments don't come often; however, when they do, they can be embraced and be a pivotal opportunity to shift, even for a few moments, from concentrating on the mundane to pondering the profound. They are critical because they turn your attention to something else, which may be an epiphany and bring enlightenment.

Sometimes planning for a celebration and enjoying achievement and milestones are valuable. Some years ago, I spent considerable time studying the importance of events, ceremonies and rituals in developing boys into men. Mainly I explored the role of rites of passage in other cultures. I concluded that these critical moments in a boy's life consist of three elements: adventure, belief and ceremony.[13]

Realizing a dream and achieving milestones towards it are important moments that help us grow and be transformed. And the moments when we stop to celebrate and reflect on what we have achieved bring the joy of accomplishment and change us. Releasing our emotion at these times – laughter, tears and shouts of happiness – serves us by emphasizing that *we did this*. We made it. We are now in a different place from where we were before.

To foster joy, be intentional. Identify waypoints or milestones along the way to celebrate your successes. Have an idea of what you want to do when you cross the finish line. Actively keep track of people, and even things, that have helped you, and find excuses to celebrate them. Remember, for every dream to come true, it takes a community of people who support you – both those close to you who provide essential support and those others who provide material and practical help.

Find reasons to celebrate and have moments to look forward to along the way.

I trust that these four steps have helped you to identify your dream, begin to realize it and to ensure that you stop and ponder each step and success along the way.

Now I would like to share with you tips and tools I have found to be helpful to me. And then in Part Four, to encourage you to meditate and reflect on profound themes relevant to you dream. To aid you, I share some stories that may feed your own dream life.

PART
THREE

TIPS AND TOOLS FOR THE JOURNEY AHEAD

Ahoy, fellow dreamers! Gather round and let me share a seafaring tale that holds wisdom for your journey towards making your dream come true.

When I acquired my boat, an exciting adventure began. But before setting sail, I received a crucial piece of advice: check the tools on board.

A boat, you see, is a marvel of intricate systems both above and below deck. Rigging, sails, steering mechanisms, engines, bilges, pumps, navigation and communications – all must work together in harmony.

To keep each component shipshape and ready for action, I needed an arsenal of tools at my disposal.

It was during a troublesome encounter with a leaking 'dripless seal' that a fellow sailor bestowed upon me some sage guidance. She had faced a similar situation and offered a brilliant solution. The fix was relatively simple, requiring specific parts and a specialized wrench, cleverly stashed in the engine room near the seal. This timely repair was critical because water invading a boat can lead to disaster in mere minutes.

Just as a sailor's toolbox is indispensable for navigating the high seas, so too do we need a dreamer's toolbox to reach our desired destinations in life. Allow me to present my 'Tips and Tools' – a treasure trove of invaluable insights, techniques and tools that have guided me on my own journey thus far.

Within my kit, you'll find an array of wisdom and practical know-how. I acquired some of these gems during my recent seafaring adventures, during which the vast ocean provided ample time for reflection on life's grand tapestry. Others, such as my 'Five Rules of Fundraising,' I have meticulously crafted and honed over six decades of experience.

Sailing, with its intricate parallels to life, offers us a marvellous metaphor. The tips and tools I share are rooted in the lessons I've learned while living on the water, yet their applicability extends far beyond maritime realms. They are tools for anyone striving to realize their dreams, navigate stormy waters or conquer the unforeseen challenges that lie ahead.

So, my fellow dreamers, open your hearts and minds as we dive into the depths. Let these tools become your faithful companions, ever at the ready to keep you on course, weather any storm and steer you towards triumph. Together, we shall uncover the secrets of success and chart a course to make our dreams a glorious reality. Anchors aweigh!

NAVIGATING LIFE

Life is a thrilling journey, but we all know the trepidation that accompanies leaving the safety of port and heading towards the unknown horizon. Yet, fear not, for there is a secret to calming the storm within – mastering the art of reading the sea and the sky.

TIP #1
MANAGING
SCARY SEAS

The sea can be scary. Embarking on the vast sea of life is unsettling too, much like setting sail into unknown waters. Understanding the ever-changing nature of the ocean is crucial, just as is comprehending the unpredictable currents and tides of life itself. Like waves crashing against the hull, various factors influence our journey, from the wind that guides us to the depths that hide beneath.

To navigate scary seas, we must acquaint ourselves with the sea's behaviour. Study its rhythms, for it has both predictable cadences and unforeseen storms. The more we learn, the more confidence we gain in our voyage.

In life, just as in sailing, the wind and waves become our teachers. However, there's more to it than judging the choppiness on the surface. It takes time to grasp the intricate workings of the sea and make informed decisions about whether to sail through turbulent waters or seek refuge in a safe harbour.

Above the surface, the wind and the moon shape the ocean's mood, while below, its depth and seabed topography play their part. Weather systems can be capricious, demanding our adaptability. We seek a predictable rhythm but must remain ready to respond to sudden changes.

The ocean has a paradox: its powerful forces are partly predictable, as seen in how the tides are dictated by the moon. Yet, external factors such as the wind and seismic activity add an element of unpredictability. Life, too, requires us to find a steady rhythm while staying agile in the face of unexpected shifts.

Just as sailors reef their sails to match the strength of the wind, we must learn to adjust our course in life, reducing our exposure to potential dangers without compromising our progress. And in extraordinary circumstances, like an incoming tsunami, we may need to defy our intuition and sail towards the swell for safety.

TIP #2
DECODING
STORMY SKIES

As we navigate the sea of life, the sky above holds valuable clues about the weather ahead, both in the atmosphere and within ourselves. By learning to read the sky and understand cloud formations, we can calm our nerves and make informed decisions about our journey.

Just like sailors who rely on their instincts and observations, we should not solely depend on predictive models but use our own eyes, ears and noses to sense the changing weather. While weather forecasting models provide measurements, nothing compares to local observations.

There is more to a weather forecast than wind, temperature and rain. The old adages hold wisdom, such as 'red sky at night, sailors' delight; red sky in the morning, sailors' warning.' These insights have stood the test of time.

To read the sky, let's explore different types of clouds, each offering warnings that can serve as metaphors for our own forecasts in our daily lives:

- **High-level clouds:** They may be beautiful but do not produce rain. They hint at approaching weather changes.
- **Mid-level clouds:** They produce some rain but not usually heavy downpours.
- **Low-level clouds (certain types):** These bring steady rain.
- **Vertical clouds:** They rise through all levels, resulting in heavy, high-volume rain over a short period.

Clouds also hold significance beyond the weather, potentially affecting our mood and mindset. For instance, when dark and foreboding clouds gather in the sky, our state of mind can quickly turn gloomy or even fearful. This parallels real-life experiences.

In her book *The Cloister Walk*, Kathleen Norris speaks of the "noonday demon," a term monks use to describe a sense of futility and meaninglessness that comes when they look towards the future. Like when clouds obscure the sun, we may feel trapped in a state of despair. To combat this, Norris discovered the power of exercise as a form of spiritual direction. By being active, moving our bodies and raising our heart rate, we redirect our mood and find renewed energy.[14]

In life, just like when we read the sky, it is important to be aware of our environment and astute in detecting potential storms. We must develop strategies to navigate through them or take action to avoid them altogether while also taking the advantage that comes with sailing at the edge of distant storms as we can harness their energy to propel us forward.

So, my fellow adventurers, let's pay attention to the sky above and within ourselves. Decode the messages it holds, adjust our course accordingly and embrace the journey, come rain or shine.

TIP #3
BUILDING A COMMUNITY: NURTURING DREAMS AND ENGAGING HEARTS

During my journey, I've discovered the immense value of forming communities around the causes that matter most to me. These communities have not only remained steadfast but also become a source of inspiration and support.

People often seek my advice about how to cultivate lasting communities around their own causes, and organizations have even hired me for this purpose. It's a privilege to guide others in this transformative process.

Why is it crucial to bring others along on your journey? Sharing your story with others allows you to refine your dream and how you articulate it to yourself. It helps you forge a network of resources, advice and support, while also providing accountability.

The remainder of the tips in this section share some invaluable lessons I've learned about building communities around causes. They explore the art of nurturing dreams, the power of effective announcements, the art of engagement, the importance of defining a critical path and how to handle critics with grace. Together these tips will help you build a community that will uplift and propel your cause forward.

TIP #4
NURTURING YOUR
DREAM PRIVATELY:
PONDER BEFORE YOU SHARE

The first step in building a community around your dream is to keep it close to your heart and nurture it privately. This period of contemplation allows your dream to germinate, evolve and gain strength. It is essential to question yourself and your commitment, ensuring that your dream is something you genuinely want to pursue. Reflect on whether your dream is a passing fancy or a deep desire that fuels your passion. This introspective phase is where dreams grow and mature.

Take my own experience with Pacific Solo, for example. The dream of crossing an ocean by sailboat had lingered in the back of my mind since my childhood. However, it seemed impossible to achieve amid the busyness and responsibilities of life, especially in Japan. But then, through a series of discoveries and opportunities, the dream resurfaced.

I nurtured it, allowing it to expand and become more precise. The goal transformed into buying a boat, living on her and sailing solo across an ocean. I pondered, questioned and cared for this dream within my soul. Only when I was certain did I start sharing it with my wife, family and close friends.

When considering your own dream and desired goals, exercise caution about announcing them too early or without proper reflection. Wait until you are certain and confident. This will allow you to surprise others with your dream's audacity, leaving them breathless. They will sense your sincerity and determination, becoming eager to follow along and provide support.

So, take the time to nurture your dream privately, allowing it to flourish. Then, when the moment is right, share it with the world and let your community gather around you, inspired by your unwavering belief.

TIP #5
SEALING YOUR COMMITMENT: THE POWER OF THE ANNOUNCEMENT

When you are certain about your audacious dream, it's crucial to carefully consider how you will share it with others. The act of announcing your dream serves as a seal of commitment, solidifying your determination to pursue it. Planning and refining your announcement can set the stage for building a supportive community.

In my own journey, I chose a significant occasion to make my announcement: my 64th birthday. Three months prior to the event, I sent out invitations to friends and family in two cities revealing that I would make three important announcements during the celebration. This allowed me additional time to fine-tune my plans and prepare for the moment.

By the time of the parties, I was fully prepared and my inner circle was aware of my intentions and was providing me with their support. The anticipation grew, so that when I made the third announcement – that I intended to buy a boat, learn how to sail and eventually cross the Pacific solo – it drew gasps of surprise. In that moment, I had gone public, and my commitment became undeniable.

The act of making this announcement triggered momentum and drew more people into my cause. As part of the announcement, I revealed a logo and a name for my endeavour, and provided a means for people to follow along. Central to this was the creation of a website where I shared my dream and plans in a concise and visually engaging manner.

Carefully consider when and how to announce your dream or cause. Choose a moment that holds significance and allows for proper preparation and refinement. Engage your inner circle of supporters beforehand so that they are ready to stand by your side. Make the announcement impactful, capturing the attention and curiosity of others. And provide a platform, such as a website or social media presence, where people can learn more and join your community.

Remember, the act of announcing your cause marks a turning point, affirming your commitment and opening doors for others to join you on your remarkable journey.

TIP #6
BUILDING YOUR DREAM TEAM:
ENGAGE AND RECRUIT
WITH ENTHUSIASM

To embark on an extraordinary journey, you need a team of supporters by your side. Engaging others and actively recruiting them to join your cause can bring your dream to life.

Imagine your dream as a grand adventure where you are the captain assembling a crew. In my case, I formed a community consisting of my family, fellow sailors, shore team and sponsors. Together, we created various platforms to keep everyone updated and engaged.

Social media can be a powerful tool for connecting with your community. Each platform attracts different individuals according to their preferences. To effectively engage with your community, take the initiative and be present on multiple platforms. Find the ways that work best for your community to engage with you.

Remember, your community is joining you because they believe in you and your dream.

Take the initiative to reach out and connect with them. Show enthusiasm, share updates and invite them to be part of your journey. By actively recruiting and engaging others, you'll create a vibrant team that propels your dream forward.

So, assemble your crew, set sail and let the spirit of adventure guide you as you engage, recruit and build a community of passionate individuals who share your vision. Together, you'll conquer challenges, celebrate victories and make your dream a reality.

TIP #7
DEFINING YOUR CRITICAL PATH AND IDENTIFYING THE ESSENTIAL CONTRIBUTORS TO YOUR SUCCESS

As your community grows, it's crucial to identify those who are essential to your project's critical path to success.

To do this, imagine your project as a complex puzzle with multiple pieces. Now, determine which pieces are essential to your success – this is your critical path.

Within my Pacific Solo team, I encountered individuals who naturally gravitated towards me, while others I actively sought out due to their specific skills and perspectives. When I acquired my boat, *Wahine*, I inherited a community that had sailed with its previous owner. These crew members were instrumental in my early days as they shared their knowledge of the boat and assisted with necessary repairs. Some of them have become long-term members of my shore team, contributing their expertise when I'm at sea.

To identify who is essential to your success, create circles within circles. Define key roles and categorize individuals based on their involvement. For example:

- Crew members who assist with repairs and improvements on the project.
- A dedicated shore team composed of experienced specialists who support you when you're actively pursuing your goals.
- Sponsors and patrons who provide financial support, making your project possible.

Recognize that even though your project may seem like an individual pursuit, it's often the collaborative efforts of a dedicated team that will drive your success.

Take time to evaluate and create your critical path. Identify those who are essential to reaching your goals and prioritize their involvement. Nurture these relationships and ensure effective communication and collaboration with these key contributors.

Remember, building a community around your cause means assembling a team of passionate individuals who align with your vision. By identifying who is essential to your critical path, you'll cultivate a strong foundation for success, propelling your project forward with the support of those who truly matter.

So, embrace the power of collaboration, define your critical path, and surround yourself with individuals who will uplift you and contribute to your journey. Together, you'll achieve remarkable feats and turn your dreams into reality.

TIP #8
RESPONDING TO CRITICS, TROLLS AND SWARMS

In the world of social media, criticism, trolls and swarms (organized groups of trolls aiming to flood your platform with negativity) are inevitable. It's essential to develop a thoughtful approach to dealing with them. Here are some suggestions based on how I like to respond to critics:

- Stay calm and 'suck it up': Expect criticism and negative input when you share your plans or ideas publicly, and embrace it as an opportunity to learn and grow.
- View each critic as a potential ally and each encounter as a chance to make friends.
- Engage with honest criticism, seeking to understand the motivations behind it and what you can learn from it.

- Use your mission and vision to explain your perspective, even to those with malicious intent.
- Check the profile and qualifications of your critics to evaluate their value and decide whether to engage with them or either ignore or block them.
- Respond with a thoughtful rebuttal or concession when warranted, showing that you value the critic's input.
- If appropriate, take action to implement what you've learned and inform the critic of the positive changes you've made. Consider inviting them to follow along on your platforms.

When dealing with potential trolls, I initially follow the same steps as for critics – specifically, embracing the opportunity to learn and evaluating the person's qualifications. However, once I start to suspect that a commenter is a troll, I shift into a slightly different gear:

- Determine whether there is any substance to the comments that you can learn from, and engage with the commenter if there is the potential for meaningful conversation.
- If they are genuinely malicious or have nothing of value to offer, then delete their comments, block them or report them.

Then there are swarms. Thankfully I have not been a victim – yet. But I know people who have. Here are some things I have learned from others' experience:

- Recognize that larger platforms may generate a higher volume of comments, making it challenging to respond to them all.
- Consider hiring someone to summarize comments and bring important ones to your attention.

- Accept that not all will like your content. Don't take it personally.

By approaching criticism, trolls and swarms with a level-headed mindset and a willingness to engage constructively, you can navigate these challenges effectively, maintain your integrity and continue building a strong community around your cause.

CREATING MOMENTUM AND ENSURING SUCCESS

Embarking on the journey of your dreams can be both exhilarating and terrifying. The fear of losing momentum, of faltering along the way, can loom like a dark cloud over your aspirations. It certainly has for me. This section of tips is aimed at helping you keep momentum.

When my story with *Wahine* started on the Island of Dreams (Yumenoshima) in Tokyo, I began to learn the power of the unexpected.

The Island of Dreams was the unlikeliest of places for my dream to gain momentum. You see, Yumenoshima is no ordinary island. It is a human-made paradise, a man-made island, made out of garbage. It stands as a resounding metaphor for what others have deemed useless and for what we ourselves may have thought worthless. Yet, these castoffs found purpose, breathing life into dreams.

It was there, amid the wonders of Yumenoshima, that I bought *Wahine*, a vessel that would carry me closer to my dreams. I moved aboard. Before that moment, my dreams existed solely within the realms of my imagination and meticulous planning. But stepping foot onto that boat changed everything. It marked the beginning of the realization of my dream and the pursuit of something grand.

Of course, the journey hasn't been without its challenges. I've had my fair share of fears and encountered failures. Yet, I've discovered the secrets to maintaining momentum, even in the face of adversity. Allow me to share them with you, fellow dreamer.

First, let's negotiate our relationship with fear and failure. Acknowledge them as companions on this extraordinary voyage, but refuse to let them steer the ship. Embrace fear as a compass that guides you towards growth and new horizons. Learn from failures, allowing them to fuel your determination and reshape your course.

Next, master the art of the pivot. Be flexible and adaptable, willing to adjust your sails when the winds of change blow. Sometimes, our initial plans may need tweaking or even a complete overhaul. Embrace these shifts, for they often lead to unexpected treasures.

Accountability is key. Hold yourself responsible for the progress of your dreams. Seek support from like-minded souls who will encourage you, challenge you and hold you accountable along the way. Together, you can weather storms and celebrate victories, keeping the momentum alive.

Finally, secure safe anchorage within your psyche and soul. Nurture your inner fire, fuelling your passion and determination. Find solace in self-care, creativity and quiet moments of reflection. Remember, dreams thrive in the fertile soil of a nurtured spirit.

So, fellow dreamer, fear not the loss of momentum. Embrace the power of discarded treasures, the unexpected turns, and the lessons learned from fear and failure. Chart your course with resilience, adaptability and accountability to yourself. And, above all, keep the flame of your dreams burning bright, anchoring your spirit to the boundless possibilities that lie ahead.

Set sail, my friend, and let the winds of your dreams carry you towards new horizons. Your own island of dreams awaits, ready to embrace you on your unique journey. Bon voyage!

TIP #9
EMBRACING FEAR
AND FAILURE

Fear and failure are not your enemies. When you are feeling blocked by an impenetrable wall, it may seem fear and failure they are the building blocks of that wall. In fact, they are companions that provoke us to find a door through that wall.

I know you already understand this – the adage that failures are an opportunity to learn is commonplace – but sometimes adages can mask our logic instead of being the logic itself. So, let me urge you to let it sink in, becoming a part of your soul and worldview. Fear and failure are our companions as we navigate through life, and this requires us to build a relationship with them. It is crucial to embrace this truth daily, especially when facing possible future failures.

I felt scared the first time I ventured out on *Wahine* alone. She was a 40-foot boat, and I had never operated one of that size before. The experience was incredible. The thrill I experienced when I took her out and brought her back safely was akin to the exhilaration of flying solo in an aeroplane for the first time. It's also similar to the feeling of climbing a rock face. You feel secure when all four limbs are in contact with the cliff, but eventually you must take one, two, three or even all four limbs off the rock to reach for the mystery above and pull yourself up.

I was terrified the first time I was instructed to walk backwards off the edge of a cliff. It defied human instinct! But I underwent training, was attached to safety ropes and had instructors guiding me. When I finally stepped back over the edge, terror engulfed me, but as I descended, I felt euphoric. I didn't want the experience to end. I would swing out from the rock face and play on it.

In these ways and so many others, fear provides a doorway through which we can exercise faith in ourselves, faith in the future and faith in the unseen forces supporting our dreams.

Write down your fears and identify the potential opportunities that lie behind them. These opportunities are the doorways you can walk through to cultivate a relationship with fear, rather than viewing fears as enemies to avoid. Make fear and failure your friends.

TIP #10
FINESSING THE ART
OF THE PIVOT

During the heights of the Covid-19 pandemic, we all came to appreciate the value of a pivot. My experiences in Part One are an apt illustration of this. When I set sail from Tokyo in March 2021, I had a goal in mind: sail to Amami Oshima and then on to Okinawa as a stress test. When, part way there, I realized that the boat and I were not ready, I pivoted to Mie Prefecture instead. I decided that I needed more experience and that I would therefore sail the coastline of

Japan for a time. But there were many more pivots to come. First, I found that Osaka Bay, where I wanted to head, was closed and would not allow me to dock. I needed to get to a port that would allow me to bring *Wahine* on land for an underwater inspection. But everyone was saying no!

Initially, it felt as if life had come to a standstill. My forward momentum was abruptly halted, and it seemed everything had been put on hold. However, it soon became apparent that the human spirit cannot be contained by a mere roadblock, no matter how insurmountable it may seem. I learned not only to adapt but also to change direction, set new goals and discover new paths in my personal and professional growth. In the end I skipped Osaka Bay and continued to sail to remote places in Japan, carrying a self-testing kit with me so I could always prove I was Covid-free to put local people at ease. Eventually I made it to a port in Kyushu that allowed me to take *Wahine* out of the water for her inspection.

The key lesson here is that obstacles do not have to impede our progress towards our goals; we simply need to adjust our plans. In fact, obstacles often hold hidden opportunities. It's an important principle that we must embrace.

Now, I want you to consider the obstacles you have encountered or anticipate facing in the future. Take a few moments to write them down. Explore different options and alternative paths that could lead you forward. While it's important to be prepared, always remember that unexpected surprises may arise along your journey, requiring you to make an immediate response.

In summary, understand that obstacles can be stepping stones to new opportunities. By being adaptable and open to change, you can navigate through any challenge that comes your way.

TIP #11
CREATING AN
ACCOUNTABILITY SYSTEM

To maintain momentum towards your dreams, it is essential to establish an accountability system. Allow me to share a personal illustration that demonstrates the power of accountability.

As I recounted in Part One, back in the year 2000 I embarked on a bicycle ride the length of Japan. Along the way, I was fortunate enough to secure a book contract with a publishing company in Oxford, UK. This external point of reference provided the extra push I needed to keep going. It taught me a valuable lesson – having external accountability can solidify our commitment and motivate us during challenging moments. It gives us the push to take that next step and continue moving forward.

Currently, my accountability lies partly with my sponsors and obligations to them. I want them to experience the benefits of my Pacific Solo dream and my collaboration with the History Channel. Although I am not obligated to fulfil their expectations, having these external accountability points proves helpful. It adds a level of responsibility to my dream and the challenges I face. While my dream may involve certain risks, the presence of accountability provides a sense of control.

Another current source of accountability is the Never Too Late Academy's investor team, with whom I have a weekly call at 5:30 on a Thursday morning. Not all join, but two or three always do. I see this call as an accountability point but also as a learning opportunity. I send out a short report 24 hours before, but the call is a conversation and the investors respond with their ideas and suggestions. I look forward to those calls.

Now, I encourage you to identify people with whom you can establish an accountability system. They don't necessarily have to be people with whom you have a formal business contract involving revenue. Your accountability system could be a personal agreement or commitment with someone you trust. By having this external point of accountability, you can ensure that you stay focused and motivated on your journey towards your dream.

TIP #13
USING RITUALS TO CEMENT YOUR COMMITMENT AND PROPEL YOURSELF FORWARD

Let's dive into the power of rituals and how they can play a crucial role in your journey. With this in mind, l invite you to consider the transformative potential of rituals to seal the deal and propel you forward.

As an illustrative example, I'll simply remind you of the power of the build-up to my 64th birthday announcement of how l planned to redesign my life. This public declaration, preceded by weeks of preparation, became a transformative ceremony that not only embedded my dream deep within my psyche but also resonated with my family, my friends and the community around me. From that moment forward, both my self-perception and the way others viewed me underwent a profound shift.

l invite you to consider what kind of ceremony or event you can organize to mark your own moment of transition. It could be a simple gathering of loved ones, a symbolic act or a public announcement that solidifies your commitment to your dream. The key is to create a powerful ritual that cements your determination and makes your aspirations tangible and real.

By incorporating a meaningful ritual into your journey, you will provide yourself with a compelling tool for staying focused and propelling yourself forward. Embrace the transformative potential of rituals and let them become a cornerstone of your path to turning your dreams into reality.

FUNDING YOUR DREAM

Let's talk about money – the gritty truth that it takes financial resources to bring a dream to life. In my own case, I faced the challenge of not having enough money, which compelled me to think deeply about how to fund my audacious and costly dream. As I embarked on this journey, my focus was on purchasing a boat, a significant milestone in the realization of my aspirations.

During my research, a trusted friend and adviser, who had already accomplished a solo endeavour himself, chuckled at my initial budget. He reminded me of the increasing costs associated with boat ownership and questioned whether I, being a pensioner with a non-profit background, had the financial means to pursue such a dream. In that moment, he suggested that I consider finding a more affordable dream – one within my financial reach.

I distinctly remember the resolute response that echoed in my mind: "No, I refuse to let the lack of money hinder me from achieving this dream. I will find a way." This unwavering determination stemmed from my belief that while money does matter, its significance is often overstated.

In the face of financial constraints, a newfound intent and willpower surged within me. I realized that there was no shame in exploring alternative avenues to fund my dream. I started contemplating creative solutions, seeking out revenue streams and embracing the idea that resourcefulness can be as valuable as monetary wealth.

In this section, we will delve into the various aspects of handling money issues when pursuing your dream. We will explore how to leverage your existing resources effectively and, if necessary, discover alternative methods to generate income streams. By sharing my experiences and insights, I hope to empower you with practical strategies and a resilient mindset so you can navigate financial challenges on your path to realizing your dreams.

Remember, while money may play a role in your journey, it should never be the sole determinant of your success. Together, let's uncover the secrets of harnessing financial resources and channelling your unwavering resolve to overcome any monetary obstacles that come your way.

TIP #14
CASH IS KING

Understanding your financial situation one week, three months and six months ahead is essential, and your cash flow report should become your daily companion.

When I embarked on my Pacific Solo journey, I had a budget in place that estimated the costs of various items and upgrades for my boat. However, I soon realized the impact of cash flow and had to prioritize wisely. I had to make tough choices, even when it came to critical equipment such as an autohelm, which in theory was indispensable (to ensure I got a good night's sleep) but which I took the tough choice to leave unrepaired (to my chagrin, as I recounted in Part One).

In the 1980s, I found myself in a challenging position as the director of finance for a medium-sized non-profit. The organization was drowning in debt, with an overdraft of nearly $1 million. It was then that I learned the invaluable lesson of the importance of cash flow. Under the guidance of a mentor who emphasized balance sheets, budgets and cash flow, and with the support of a vigilant bank manager, I began submitting weekly cash-flow reports.

Every Friday morning, I gathered my team to assess our revenue for the upcoming week and strategize about how we would pay our bills. Through perseverance and careful financial management, we managed to pay off the overdraft and emerge from a dire situation. This experience ingrained in me the understanding that without sufficient cash, it becomes nearly impossible to fund your dreams.

Cash is indeed king. I urge you to create a cash-flow report and revisit it regularly, at least monthly. Keep in mind that your dream's timeline may be subject to adjustments, but it's crucial to ensure you have enough cash to achieve each milestone along the way. Figure 1 shows examples of how I budgeted and mapped out my cash needs for my own journey. Take a look and start building your own cash-flow plan.

Remember, as you consider your future cash needs, to take advantage of the valuable strategies outlined in the next few tips. Stay optimistic and proactive in seeking opportunities to support your vision.

With a well-managed cash flow and a determined mindset, you will be one step closer to transforming your dreams into reality. Keep pushing forward, knowing that financial obstacles can be overcome with careful planning and resourcefulness.

TIP #15
THE FIVE RULES OF FUNDRAISING: UNLEASHING THE POWER OF CONNECTIONS

Fundraising has been a significant part of my life for over 55 years. It all started when I was just 12 years old and I participated in the charity walk Miles for Millions, as I described in Part One. Throughout my journey, I've discovered five invaluable rules that have shaped my success in raising funds. These rules are not mere tips; they form an action sequence that can transform your life and help you to secure the support you need to bring your dreams to fruition.

RULE 1

Make a list, but not just any list. When seeking funds or sponsors, start by creating a comprehensive list of individuals and organizations that have the means to contribute or have access to resources that can be classified as expenses. Initially, it may seem daunting, but,you'll be surprised at how many names you can come up with. Then, categorize each name based on various factors, such as their financial capacity, accessibility, brand alignment (yours and theirs) and desirability meaning your desire to work with them or now. For example, there may be a family member with the means, the accessibility and they share your vision, but family politics would be affected. This strategic approach will allow you to prioritize and focus your efforts effectively.

RULE 2

Craft a compelling pitch deck and tell your story. Your story is the heart of your fundraising efforts. Clearly and concisely explain your mission, what you hope to achieve and, most importantly, who will benefit from your endeavours. A pitch deck is a powerful tool to communicate your ideas and get potential sponsors excited about supporting you. It provides an overview of your project or business plan, showcasing your products, services and growth traction. Highlight what sponsors can expect to gain from their association with you, considering their specific desires – whether that's social media rights, product placement or brand alignment.

RULE 3

Master the art of the ask. When it's time to request financial support, remember three crucial elements. First, be clear and specific about what you are asking for. Second, adapt your asking approach to suit the cultural norms of your audience. Different regions may respond better to different levels of directness and softness. Lastly, once you've made your ask, allow space for their response. Avoid filling awkward silences and listen attentively to their reply.

RULE 4

Respect their decision. Whether the answer is a definite no or a maybe (or even an immediate yes!), it's crucial to accept it. Thank them for their time and consideration. If it's a no, do not try to persuade them otherwise. If it's a maybe, inquire whether there is any additional information or support you can provide to help them reach a decision. Sometimes, their response will reveal opportunities for creative solutions within the framework of your sponsorship plan. For example, a friend told me that he wanted to sponsor but the amount he was authorized to spend was lower than the tiers I had outlined. The outcome was that we agreed for that amount his company would have social media rights to use my journey in their own company blog to inspire staff and customers, etc.

RULE 5

Foster a sense of community. Regardless of their response, offer options for ongoing engagement and connection. Invite them to join your mailing list, follow you on social media or participate in other activities that allow them to stay in touch and be part of your vibrant community. Building relationships and maintaining connections is vital for long-term success.

In conclusion, be creative and respectful, and most of all be mindful that you do not want to burn bridges. Rather you want to nurture long-term relationships. Take brand alignment seriously and seek to understand how your story can connect with theirs. Sometimes opportunities will come to you through friends and connections who are genuinely interested in what you're doing. When these opportunities arise, honour the terms and conditions, demonstrate flexibility and act with integrity.

By applying these five rules, you can unleash the power of connections and secure the support you need to turn your dreams into reality.

TIP #16
CHOOSING A
CROWDFUNDING PLATFORM

Crowdfunding has emerged as an effective way to raise funds for projects and initiatives. However, it is essential to recognize that not all crowdfunding platforms are the same. Each platform has its own set of pros and cons, and understanding these differences is crucial in selecting the right one for your fundraising goals.

In this tip, I will provide an overview of the crowdfunding platforms I have personally used (with the exception of Crowdfunder, which I have looked into but not actually used), discussing their unique features, advantages and considerations.

KICKSTARTER
Kickstarter is a well-established platform known for showcasing creative projects and innovative ideas. It offers a robust community of backers who are eager to support unique ventures. One of the main advantages of Kickstarter is its all-or-nothing funding model, where you must reach your funding goal to receive any funds. This can help to create a sense of urgency and motivate supporters. However, it's important to note that Kickstarter focuses primarily on creative projects, and it may be challenging to gain traction for other types of initiative.

INDIEGOGO
Indiegogo is another popular crowdfunding platform but it offers more flexibility in terms of project types. It allows both all-or-nothing and flexible funding options, giving fundraisers the choice to keep the funds even if the goal is not reached. Indiegogo has a global user base and offers extensive

support and resources for campaign creators. Keep in mind that the platform operates on a fee structure, and fees may vary depending on the funding type and campaign results.

GoFundMe

GoFundMe is widely recognized as a source of funding for personal and charitable causes. It provides a user-friendly interface and allows for quick setup, making it an accessible platform for individuals seeking immediate assistance. GoFundMe's fees include a percentage of each donation you receive. While it is a popular platform, it's important to consider that the broad range of campaigns and causes can make it challenging to stand out.

PATREON

Patreon is a unique crowdfunding platform that focuses on ongoing support for creators, such as artists, musicians, writers and content creators. It allows fans and supporters to contribute regular payments in exchange for exclusive content or perks. Patreon provides a space for creators to build a loyal community and receive sustained support. However, it is more suitable for individuals or entities consistently producing content than for one-time projects.

CROWDFUNDER

Crowdfunder is a platform that specializes in equity crowdfunding, connecting startups and small businesses with potential investors. It provides opportunities for individuals to invest in early-stage companies and receive equity in return. Crowdfunder operates on a fee structure based on the amount raised. If you have a business or startup seeking investment, Crowdfunder can be a valuable platform to explore.

Please note that the information provided about each platform is based on my personal experience and understanding. It's important to conduct thorough research and consider your specific project's nature, goals and target audience when choosing a crowdfunding platform. Each platform has its own unique community, features and fee structure, so selecting the one that aligns best with your needs and objectives is essential for a successful crowdfunding campaign. The following suggestions will help you to make an informed decision:

- **Define your fundraising goals:** Clearly articulate what you aim to achieve through crowdfunding. Is it for a creative project, a personal cause, a business venture or ongoing content creation? Understanding your goals will help you align with the right platform.
- **Research and compare platforms:** Take the time to explore various crowdfunding platforms beyond the ones mentioned here. Look for platforms that cater to your specific project type and audience. As suggested above, consider factors such as funding models (all-or-nothing vs. flexible), fee structures, user base and success stories.
- **Analyse each platform's features:** Evaluate the features and tools offered by each platform. Consider aspects such as campaign setup, customization options, community engagement, social sharing capabilities and support resources. Choose a platform that provides the necessary features to enhance your campaign's visibility and engagement.
- **Study success stories and campaigns:** Look for successful campaigns similar to yours on each platform. Analyse their strategies, messaging, visuals and supporter engagement. Learning from existing campaigns can provide valuable insights and inspiration for your own fundraising journey.

- **Consider your target audience:** Reflect on your intended audience and their preferred crowdfunding platform, especially where your potential backers are most likely to engage and contribute. By selecting a platform aligned with your target audience's preferences, you increase the likelihood of attracting supporters.
- **Review the fee structure:** Understand the fee structure of each platform, including any transaction fees, processing fees and platform commissions. Consider how these fees will impact your fundraising goals and budget. Keep in mind that while some platforms charge fees, they may offer additional features and support that can enhance your campaign's success.
- **Plan your campaign strategy:** Develop a comprehensive strategy for your crowdfunding campaign. This includes setting realistic funding goals, creating a compelling pitch, designing engaging visuals, outlining rewards or perks, and planning a promotional strategy to reach your target audience.
- **Launch and engage:** Once you've selected the ideal crowdfunding platform, it's time to launch your campaign. Regularly engage with your supporters, provide updates and express gratitude for contributions. Actively promote your campaign through social media, email newsletters and other marketing channels.

Remember, success in crowdfunding requires effort, persistence and effective communication. Continuously adapt your strategy based on the feedback and engagement you receive from your supporters. By carefully selecting the right crowdfunding platform and implementing a well-thought-out campaign plan, you can maximize your chances of reaching your fundraising goals and bringing your project or cause to life.

TIP #17
USING YOUR OWN
MONEY JUDICIOUSLY

Using your own money to fund your dream project can be a viable option if you have cash to spare, but it requires careful consideration and planning. In my case I had limited cash, but I ploughed everything I had into my project before asking others. I sought the advice of others, including serial entrepreneurs, a banker and a lawyer. Following is what I learned and have found helpful:

- **Decide whether your project is a hobby or a business:** Consider its long-term potential and the financial implications involved. If it's a hobby, you may not expect financial returns but can still enjoy the process and contribute to society. However, if your goal is to start a business, think about scalability and how you can generate returns for yourself, your family and those who have supported you.

- **Assess your resources:** Create two budgets – an essential budget and an ideal budget. The essential budget should include the minimum items you need to get started, while the ideal budget should encompass everything you would like to have funded. For both budgets, list the personal assets you are willing to commit and the sacrifices you are prepared to make.

- **Determine a realistic budget:** Review both budgets and come up with a realistic middle ground that includes the necessary items for your success along with any optional items you can afford or are willing to secure through raising funds. This will allow you to evaluate your external funding needs.

- **Stick with your budget:** Once you have determined the amount you are willing to commit from your own funds, ensure you devote 100% of that money to your cause. This is especially important if you have backers, to show respect for their contributions.

• **Reflect your values and ethics:** Share your project with others and let them know who you are and what you stand for. Align everything you do with your values to ensure your dream and plan is a reflection of your character. When people see your commitment and integrity, they will be more inclined to support you.

By approaching self-funding with a clear budget, staying true to your values and effectively communicating your mission, you can leverage your own resources wisely and create a foundation for success.

TIP #18
GOING FIRST CLASS
IS SECOND RATE

In this final tip about funding your dream, I want to emphasize an important concept: dreams need not be expensive. Let's explore why and how you can apply this mindset.

Many people believe that pursuing their dreams requires significant financial resources, but that's not always the case.

Here's why: your will is more powerful than your wallet. The power of choice and determination can bring your dreams to life. By making a firm decision, creating a plan and exerting your will, you can achieve seemingly impossible goals. Trust in your ability to manifest what you desire and take action towards it.

This is why going first class is second rate. Engaging in extravagant and expensive experiences may seem desirable, but true fulfilment often lies in simplicity. Living modestly while pursuing your dreams can bring unexpected joys and meaningful connections. Embrace the essence of your journey rather than focusing solely on material comforts.

It's important to acknowledge the role of money, how to spend it wisely and how to generate income. However, it's equally crucial to guard against greed and remember that true happiness doesn't always come from a luxurious lifestyle.

Here's what you can do to apply this mindset:

- **Embrace the power of your will:** Make a conscious decision to pursue your dreams and believe in your ability to make them a reality. Develop a plan of action and commit to it wholeheartedly.
- **Emphasize experiences over material possessions:** Focus on the richness of your journey rather than on accumulating expensive belongings. Find joy in simplicity and meaningful interactions with others who share similar passions.
- **Be mindful of your spending:** While money plays a role, assess your expenses and prioritize wisely. Invest in what truly matters for your dream project or venture, and avoid unnecessary extravagance.

Similarly, by making conscious decisions aligned with your dreams, you may forgo short-term luxuries in exchange for long-term fulfilment and opportunities.

So, as you embark on your dream pursuit, remember that it's not always about buying high-ticket items or living lavishly. Embrace simplicity, nurture your willpower and focus on the essence of your journey. The path to fulfilling your dreams can be within reach, regardless of financial constraints.

YOUR MINDSET TOOLBOX

It's always handy to have a treasure trove of tools and tips at your disposal. Just like my trusty tool bag on the boat filled with odd bits and spare gadgets, a collection of miscellaneous resources can come to the rescue when unexpected moments arise and require a swift reaction or a mindset repair. These tools can help you to keep your mindset in tip-top working condition:

- **The Perspective Prism:** When the waves of doubt or negativity threaten to overshadow your vision, reach for the Perspective Prism. This magical device helps you to view situations from different angles, revealing new insights and possibilities. Twist it, turn it and watch your perspective expand in the most delightful ways.

- **The Resilience Ratchet:** Life's challenges can sometimes feel like a stubborn nut that refuses to crack. But fear not! With the Resilience Ratchet in your toolkit, you'll be able to steadily turn the handle of perseverance. Each click brings you closer to overcoming obstacles and unlocking the sweet taste of success.

- **The Mindfulness Multitool:** In the fast-paced whirlwind of dreams, it's easy to lose touch with the present moment. That's where the Mindfulness Multitool comes in. With its versatile features of breath awareness, grounding exercises and gratitude prompts, it helps you to anchor yourself in the now and savour the beauty of each passing breeze.

- **The Imagination Wrench:** Sometimes, all it takes is a little twist of imagination to fix a glitch in your mindset. Reach for the Imagination Wrench and watch as it effortlessly loosens the bolts of self-limiting beliefs, allowing your creativity to flow freely. With this tool in hand, there's no problem you can't unscrew and reimagine.

Remember, the key is to have these tools readily available in your mental toolbox. Keep them close by and, when unexpected moments arise, reach in and pick the perfect tool to refine, repair or revolutionize your mindset. Let the journey be enjoyable, filled with laughter and a sense of adventure as you unlock the potential within.

Following are some further tips that you can use alongside these tools to give yourself a mindset boost when you need it.

TIP #19
UNLEASH THE POWER
OF SWEARING:
SHAKE THE UNIVERSE
WITH THE RIGHT WORD

There's an art to swearing and even the judicious use of the infamous F-bomb can transform an experience and shift your mindset in a positive direction. Allow me to share what I learned from my son, my mother and a theologian about the power of the right word at the right time.

Picture this: my son convinced me to try snowboarding when I was in my forties and he was just a 12-year-old daredevil. Now, I had always stuck to skiing, but I decided to give snowboarding a shot. Long story short, I had a disastrous collision with a mogul, resulting in a shattered shoulder. Ouch!

I nursed myself down to the ski patrol and they attempted to fix my dislocated shoulder. But alas, they failed, deeming my foreigner status and 'being a guy' gene to be the culprits. Off to the hospital I went, where I discovered my shoulder was completely busted apart. It required a ten-day stay and an operation to put the pieces back together.

Now, here comes the juicy part. Before this incident, I had been coaching my 12-year-old son, Ryan, on the nuances of swear words. Rather than simply saying, "Don't swear," we had embarked on a journey to understand the severity and appropriate usage of different words. We had discussed how my preacher father, despite his religious background, would occasionally use strong language to describe despicable things, but only in the right context.

I had shared with Ryan the story of a theologian friend who explained, citing Old Testament references, that sometimes, in the face of injustice and abuse, there may be a justifiable moment to unleash a powerful "fuck you." However, I emphasized the need for judicious use of such language.

Fast forward to my hospital stay following the accident. My son approached me and asked, "Dad, which word can we use now?" I chuckled and suggested sticking to a milder expression, such as "damn."

My mother, Greta, knew the art. She has saved certain words for the right moment but the F-bomb she has only used once her life.

Now 94 years old, she has a fear of the third floor in her retirement village, which she affectionately calls the "floor for crazies" (it is actually for those needing more care). She dreads the thought of being moved there, but it could only happen if recommended by a doctor. So, every few months, she faces a memory test, knowing the weight it holds and the potential consequences.

During one of these tests, the lady administering it asked my mother to name words starting with the letter "F." And you can guess what happened next. My mother, in her nervous state, blurted out, "Father, forgive" as her first response. Then, after a momentary pause, she exclaimed "failure." But then, something extraordinary occurred. My mother became animated, stood up straight and passionately uttered, "Here's one for you: FUCK FUCK FUCK FUCK YOU!"

Now, let me be clear. It shocked us all, especially considering my mother's reputation as the wife of a minister and her general avoidance of expletives. But you know what? It was entirely appropriate for her to say it in that moment of losing control, reclaiming her power and asserting herself against the forces that threatened her.

So, here's the tip, my fearless companions: when things get rough, when life throws its worst at you, give vent to your emotions. Find the appropriate word, the strongest one for that very moment, and address the universe with unapologetic vigour. Embrace the release, enjoy every second and relish the moment of mindset recalibration.

TIP #20
MEN BE MEN
(I MAY GET INTO TROUBLE
FOR THIS ONE)

I am compelled to address an important topic: men in our society. While I acknowledge that men and women share many common traits, it is clear that there are differences between the genders, particularly at the extremes. In light of these differences, I invite you to consider a code of manhood derived from Japanese culture: the Samurai code.

Let me share an enlightening experience I had during my travels. I visited a remote inlet on Amami Oshima, where sumo wrestling thrives among small communities. Within these communities, a unique rite of passage caught my attention. When boys turn 15, they are expected to lift a 'strength stone' and proclaim, "I am now a man!" This tradition embodies a powerful symbolism of responsibility and growth.

I am aware that discussing men's issues can be controversial in today's climate, but I believe it is essential to provide guidance and inspiration to those who seek meaning in their lives. Men need responsibility to find purpose, just as lifting a load brings significance to their existence. However, when that responsibility loses meaning, despair can set in.

It is disheartening that older men in Western culture often face distrust and suspicion. While I don't claim to fully understand this perspective, I believe we can draw insights from the Bushido Code of the Samurai. Originally studied by economist Inazō Nitobe in his book *Bushido: The Soul of Japan* (1899), this code highlights qualities such as rectitude, courage, benevolence, politeness, honesty, sincerity, honour, loyalty, character and self-control.[15]

Men, I implore you to dare to dream. Embrace your unique journey and step off the paths of conformity to realize a future aligned with your aspirations. By adopting the traits exemplified in the Samurai code, you can cultivate your own leadership qualities and find meaning in your endeavours.

I understand that, in the past, addressing men directly has been met with criticism and accusations of sexism. Yet, I cannot shake the concern that some men struggle to mature and take responsibility. While boys and girls share common traits as humans, it is important to acknowledge the distinct experiences and challenges each gender faces.

Throughout my writing journey, I have kept men like myself in mind. I have witnessed unfair stigmatization of men as a collective, even though it is only a small fraction of individuals who engage in predatory and exploitative behaviour. We must remember that both men and women have the potential for great good and great harm, and we must strive to create a balanced and equitable society.

Embrace the qualities of the Samurai code. Dare to dream, and step away from conformity to pursue your aspirations. Find meaning in shouldering responsibilities and lifting the load that brings purpose to your life.

Remember, this tip is primarily intended for men, but its principles of personal growth and character development can resonate with anyone seeking fulfilment and purpose.

TIP #21
EXPAND YOUR
VOCABULARY FOR
PRECISION AND POWER

Words possess an incredible power that is often underestimated and underutilized. When used loosely and without thought, words can convey insincerity, confusion and a lack of trust. However, when wielded with precision, they become potent tools capable of making a lasting impact.

Go back to Exercise 2 (in Part Two, Step 2) and, if you haven't done it already, give it a go. I use this exercise in my Personal Mission Statement classes to enhance the participants' appreciation of words and inspire a desire to expand their vocabulary. It is fun in a group because we pass pieces of paper around and try to guess who wrote which words. When the person is revealed, they explain why. But you can do it on your own too.

Once you've completed this exercise, challenge yourself to incorporate your three newly discovered words – one that you like, one that you've heard recently and one that's brand new to you – into your vocabulary at least three times over the next five days. This practice will foster attentiveness towards new words and ignite a hunger within you to expand your lexicon. The goal is to develop greater precision in your thinking, speaking and writing.

By engaging in this exercise, you will unlock the full potential of words, harnessing their precision and impact to express yourself more effectively and cultivate trust and understanding in your interactions with others.

TIP #22
EMBRACE FEAR
OF FAILURE
AS YOUR ALLY

Fear of failure is a familiar companion that often lurks in the shadows of our minds. Tip #9 looked specifically at how failure and fear can act as doors to growth and transformation. Following are some specific tools you can use to acknowledge and overcome fear of failure when you feel its holding you back in your pursuit of an immediate goal. Together, these ideas encourage you to shift your state of mind and embrace fear as your ally:

- Engage in physical exercise to energize your body and mind, and break free from the clutches of stagnation.
- Embrace novelty and do something different. Step out of your comfort zone and explore uncharted territories, expanding your horizons.
- Immerse yourself in profound and uplifting literature before you drift off to sleep. Let the wisdom of great minds inspire and nourish your soul.
- Confront the critical voices within yourself and from others. Rather than dismissing or ignoring them, or worse reacting to them and consider is their some value in them. Tough skin is needed at times like this, and it could just spur you towards improvement.
- Remember, you are in control of your own destiny. Take full responsibility for the decisions you make, refusing to burden others with the weight of your choices.
- As I previously shared, learn the art of swearing. Sometimes, in the face of critics, fears and self-doubt, you need to stand tall, straighten your posture and boldly declare to these voices: "Fuck you."

By implementing these practices, you can transform your relationship with fear, turning it into a catalyst for personal growth and resilience. Embracing fear as a friend allows you to navigate the challenges ahead with a sense of empowerment and purpose.

By embracing fear and turning it into your ally, you can unlock hidden potential, conquer challenges, and achieve personal and professional growth beyond your wildest dreams. So, step forward with courage and let fear become the wind beneath your wings on the journey to success.

TIP #23
EMBRACE THE
MYSTERY OF LIFE
AND BELIEVE IN
POSSIBILITY

Life is a journey that often fills us with doubt. We witness suffering, injustice and inequality, and we experience personal loss and heartache. These moments of doubt can shake our beliefs, but they don't have to lead us to disbelief or atheism. Instead, they can guide us towards a different kind of belief – a belief in the mystery of life and the endless possibilities it holds.

I was born into a world of dogma, where beliefs were handed down to me. But as I traversed through life, doubt seeped in, triggered by the struggles I saw others endure and witnessing tragedies within my own family . Yet, rather than resulting in me losing faith, my doubt fuelled a deeper belief – a belief in the unknown, in what lies beyond our comprehension. I came to accept that there are many things I cannot and will not understand.

The teachings of my preacher father still resonate within me, and I hope they hold true. However, I live in a perpetual state of awe, humbled by the mysteries of life, the vastness of the universe and the concept of eternity.

My quest to live on the sea and experience Nemo North, a place of solitude and contemplation (see Part One), is not driven by a need to prove or learn anything. It is fuelled by an insatiable desire to witness, to experience and to truly live. It is a journey that takes me to a place of profound ignorance, where I gaze upon the expanse of the heavens, knowing I can never reach its depths. It is an exploration of the mysteries within my own soul, where my deepest thoughts reside, and a cautious acknowledgement of the potential darkness that lies below, ever reminding me to tread carefully.

To apply this tip in your own life, I encourage you to:

- **Embrace the mystery of life:** Instead of seeking concrete answers for everything, allow yourself to revel in the beauty of the unknown and the limitless possibilities it holds.
- **Believe in possibility:** Cultivate a mindset that acknowledges that anything is possible, even in the face of uncertainty and doubt.
- **Live with awe and humility:** Maintain a sense of wonder and reverence for the mysteries of life, the vastness of the universe and the eternal nature of existence.

By embracing the mystery and holding on to belief in possibility, you can approach life with a sense of curiosity, wonder and openness. Embracing the unknown allows you to embrace the richness of the human experience and embark on a profound journey of self-discovery. So, let go of the need for absolute certainty, and instead embrace the enigma that is life itself.

BONUS:
TEN NEW TIPS TO CHANGE THE COURSE OF YOUR LIFE

In my book *Never Too Late*, which was published over a decade ago, I presented ten tips to help readers change the course of their lives.[16] In 2022, after experiencing an accident at sea that necessitated a rescue tow by the Coast Guard, I found myself stuck with my boat for a few weeks on a remote island. During this time, I had ample opportunity to reflect and reconsider the ten themes and tips from my book. As a result, I compiled a revised list of ten tips to share with you. Take a moment to read through them and pay attention to any thoughts or insights they evoke:

1. **Navigation:** Embrace multiple maps to navigate your journey. (Original: Get a Map)
2. **Love:** Cultivate self-love to amplify your capacity to love others. (Original: Locate Love and Find Authenticity)
3. **Endurance:** Embrace the sweat as a sign of progress and victory. (Original: Discover the Power of Perseverance)
4. **Geography:** Transform your surroundings and experience the transformative power of change. (Original: Change Places and Be Renewed)

5. **Money:** Unleash your creativity and explore diverse avenues for generating income, including becoming a digital nomad. (Original: Money Matters but Not as Much as You Think)

6. **Fitness:** Take time to cleanse not just your body but also your mind, like a refreshing bath. (Original: Supersize Your Life, not Your Body)

7. **Curves:** Embrace uncertainty and the beauty of life's twists and turns. (Original: Straight-Line Lives are Boring)

8. **Service:** Avoid becoming a 'servaholic' by allowing others to serve you. (Original: Serve Others and Reap the Rewards)

9. **Soulcraft:** Dive deep into profound moments and expand your connection to the sacred. (Original: Touch the Sacred and Tend the Soul)

10. **Time:** Recognize that not every hour is created equal and be mindful of how you spend it. (Original: Stop Watching TV)

I hope these additional tips will serve as a valuable addition to your toolbox. Good luck on your journey of self-discovery and transformation.

The following, final part of this book presents a collection of readings and stories designed to ignite thought and reflection. Enjoy the process and keep dreaming on!

PART FOUR

DAILY
READINGS
AND
REFLECTIONS

Reflection is the key that unlocks the door to profound insights, resolves lingering issues and takes us on an adventure into the depths of our own thoughts.

In this part of the book, you have the freedom to immerse yourself in stories, reflections and exercises. Think of the reflections as stepping stones to ignite your imagination and trigger contemplation. They are carefully selected readings, hand picked to spark your mind and set your thoughts in motion. As you dive into each tale, allow your mind to wander, and embrace the thoughts that come alive within you.

But hold on: there is a twist to make this experience even more memorable and fun. My intention is for you to return to the readings multiple times in a kind of cycle. However, inspired by a seasoned sailor's secret method for spicing up long passages, I have organized the readings into an eight-day week instead of the usual seven days. Why? Well, just like that sailor, who wanted to avoid the monotony of associating specific days with particular meals, we're breaking free from routine and injecting excitement into the cycle. Get ready for a new kind of week that keeps things fresh and intriguing!

Now, here's a pro tip for maximizing the value of each reading: keep a journal by your side. After diving into each story, take a moment to let your thoughts flow onto the pages. Write down the insights, reflections and questions that arise within you. Then, as you progress to the second week, revisit the readings and your previous notes. Add new thoughts and observations, building upon the foundation you've already established. Repeat this process once more in the third week, delving deeper into your evolving reflections.

But wait, there's even more! If you're feeling ambitious and eager to extract the most from this exercise, here's an additional challenge for the fourth and final week. Take your accumulated notes and transform them into captivating stories of your own. Write them down or grab a mic and record your voice as you share the highlights of your reflections. Let your imagination run wild and capture the essence of your journey in compelling narratives.

If you immerse yourself in this delightful cycle of readings, reflections and revelations – allowing your mind to wander and embracing the thoughts that come alive within you – you may just experience some magical moments.

So, let's go.

READING #1:
THINK–FEEL–DO

Here are three seemingly ordinary words that, when fused together, become an extraordinary force. These words hold the key to unlocking a transformative concept, a holistic prescription for your redesigned life. So, let us delve into the power of these words: think, feel, do.

Think. Feel. Do. Alone, they hold significance, but together, they form a powerful way to live. Think of them as the pillars that uphold the architecture of your existence. When you blend any two of these words, you equip yourself with invaluable tools that you can use to construct a fulfilling life. Yet, when you synergize all three, you awaken a superpower within.

Pause for a moment and reflect on which of these words resonates with you the most. We all engage in thinking, feeling and doing, but there may be a leaning – an inclination – that defines us. Are you a thinker, embracing the power of reason and intellect? Or perhaps you're a feeler, attuned to emotions and driven by empathy? Maybe you identify as a doer, a catalyst for change who embraces action above all else?

Assign a number, on a scale of 0 to 10, to each of these traits to uncover the depths of your unique composition. Some lean towards the cerebral, lost in thoughts but wary of emotions and hesitant to act. Others are sensitive souls, effortlessly empathizing with the world and its joys and sorrows. And then there are the action-driven individuals, the catalysts for transformation.

Regardless of where you find yourself on this matrix, I invite you to ponder how you can strengthen the other aspects of your being. If you are a thinker, explore ways to tap into your emotions, embracing the profound highs and lows of life. If you are a feeler, challenge yourself to engage in deep thinking and translate your insights into practical action. And if you are a doer, consider infusing your actions with empathy and thoughtful reflection, so as to shape a more profound impact on the world around you.

This journey of integration requires discipline. It calls upon you to develop your strength in all three dimensions, allowing them to harmonize within you.

Embrace the fusion of these three words, allowing them to intertwine and shape your journey. As you embark on this transformative path, let these words guide you, igniting the power within. Embrace the thinker, the feeler and the doer within you, for they hold the key to unlocking the extraordinary life you dare to dream.

READING #2:
MY FIRST KISS (IT WAS SCARY!)

Life has taught me an invaluable lesson: fear is not our foe but rather a dance partner with whom we must tango. Think of it as stepping onto the dance floor of a new experience, where fear becomes the rhythm that guides our footsteps. I have a tale to share – a story about my first kiss – that perfectly encapsulates the profound truth that, sometimes, 'love' or to 'care' deeply about the outcome, can be downright scary.

Let me tell you about the first time I kissed Kande, my wife. Of course, back then, she wasn't my wife yet, but rather a fascinating person who had captivated my heart. We shared the same group of friends, and one fateful evening at a party, I overheard her mentioning that she wouldn't allow a boy to kiss her unless he asked for permission first. That titbit of information sparked a gleam of inspiration within me.

With utmost care, I planned the perfect setting for our potential kiss. We had spent time together, gone on a few dates and held hands on occasion. Our connection was blossoming. So, one Sunday evening, I mustered up the courage and suggested a stroll in Stanley Park (in Vancouver, British Columbia,

Canada) to witness the submarine races. There was, of course, no such thing, but Kande, being quite perceptive, knew I was leading up to something and eagerly agreed, supposedly curious about these underwater races she had never seen before.

As we wandered along the park's seawall, she eventually asked the obvious question, "Where are the submarines?" I smiled, not surprised by her query, and responded, "Well, you see, when submarines race, they remain submerged, so let's take a walk instead." And walk we did, immersing ourselves in the beauty of Stanley Park. Eventually we found ourselves near the Totem Poles, softly made radiant by the moon's glow – a moment of perfect timing and ambiance.

Then came the crucial moment. I tried to muster up the nerve to ask if I could kiss her. But right then and there, fear slithered into my thoughts. What if she said no? The hours of rehearsing in front of the mirror gave way to a sudden surge of trepidation. I had dreamed of her surrendering to my embrace, but the possibility of rejection loomed over me, threatening to shatter my hopes of a long-lasting connection.

Nevertheless, I found the courage and asked the question that could change everything. And to my relief, she replied with a resounding yes. As for the rest of that evening's story – well, I'll keep that between me and Kande!

I share this tale not only for its amusement value but also as a gentle reminder of how fear can stealthily creep into our dreams. It often catches us off guard. However, when we confront fear head on and pass through its daunting doorway, we find ourselves stepping into the promised land of new possibilities.

I invite you to reflect on your own dreams. What is it that scares you? What if the outcome wasn't as you envisioned? Take a moment to embrace the exhilarating dance between fear and care. Remember that sometimes, in the midst of our fears, is where we discover our deepest desires and dreams.

READING #3:
SILENCE VS. SOLITUDE

The book *Sailing to the Edge of Time* states a profound truth: "Ocean passages are exercises in management. You manage provisions, water, fuel, and most importantly, your psyche."[17] This quote resonates deeply with me as I mentally prepare myself for months alone at sea when I again attempt my Pacific Solo voyage.

Once, during my regular breakfast gatherings with friends in Tokyo, the topic emerged of transformative journeys on Vispanna Silent Retreats. Three of my friends shared their experiences, suggesting that I embark on a silent retreat to prepare for my upcoming trip. However, I realized that it wasn't practice in silence I needed, as the challenge ahead wasn't coping with the absence of sound but rather the absence of companionship. It is solitude that awaits me in the middle of the Pacific Ocean.

Undoubtedly, the endeavour I have set for myself is daunting in numerous ways. There is much preparation and learning ahead – acquiring necessary skills, building physical strength to navigate the boat and developing the mental resilience to go solo.

Vito Dumas, in his book *Alone through the Roaring Forties*, remarks, "It is out there at sea that you are truly yourself."[18] To be honest, this aspect of the journey frightens me the most – the prospect of being alone with my own thoughts.

Through extensive research, H. R. Matthew explored the effects of solitude on solo sailors and made an intriguing discovery. Solitary wanderers often find it challenging to express their inner struggles, as such self-revelation is not typically aligned with the hero ethic prevalent in Anglo-Saxon culture. Repression becomes the norm. However, spending time alone at sea triggers a process where the unconscious mind becomes activated, unearthing repressed emotions as hallucinations.[19]

It may sound peculiar, perhaps even a little eccentric, but I yearn to be alone with my essential self. I crave a prolonged period of silence. I seek to learn and understand whether I truly exist, as Pablo Neruda so eloquently expressed.[20]

Yes, silence will likely dominate my journey – the suppression of voices, including my own. While I will have a radio and audiobooks at my disposal, I intend to use them sparingly. I fear they might disrupt the sacred symphony of the sea and the wind, which possess a unique language through which they communicate with me.

In the era of social distancing and solitude brought about by the Covid-19 pandemic, I was reminded of my good fortune in having a sailboat and a log house on a mountainside as my home. Others endured far more confinement and loneliness. My 91-year-old mother, for instance, suffered intense solitude, confined to her small room for weeks on end. Each time she dared to peek outside, she told me that a booming voice scolded her: "Get back in your room!" I hold immense respect and love for people like her.

Over the course of the pandemic, I contemplated the challenges of isolation, seclusion, solitude and loneliness.

These are the very things that can drive sailors to madness, I have been told. Hallucinations, voices and nightmares are common for solo sailors, I have read. To be frank, the prospect of being alone in the middle of the North Pacific is unsettling at best and terrifying at times.

In preparation for my journey, I have noted three horizons I plan to view – not only to survive my two or three months of solitude but also to thrive. I encourage you to make use of them too.

- **Horizon #1:** Look to the distant large horizon and ponder the profound. Each porthole on my boat offers a slightly different perspective on the outside world. Each presents an opportunity to contemplate a horizon larger than my confined space. In these views, I find inspiration and possibilities.

- **Horizon #2:** Look to the near and tiny horizon and search for the magical. I am rediscovering the joy of exploration and adventure within the limited space of my boat. Xavier de Maistre, in his book *Voyage Around My Room*, chronicled his travels around his room while he was confined for six weeks.[21] His perspective transformed a small space into a universe to be explored. By embracing a similar mindset, I can find magic even in the smallest details.

- **Horizon #3:** Look at the inner horizon and search for comedy. Laughter is a powerful catalyst for change. It alters our attitudes and brings us joy. In preparing for my voyage, most of my learning has come from failure. Sometimes, my mistakes are so absurd that I can't help but laugh at myself. And there are moments of pure joyous laughter when I conquer a problem I initially deemed insurmountable. Laughter uplifts the soul and spreads throughout our lives.

As you reflect on the profound notions of silence and solitude, consider the moments of solitude in your own life, whether intentional or unexpectedly encountered. How does silence impact your psyche? Do you find it challenging or liberating? How might you incorporate more moments of silence into your daily routine to nourish your soul and deepen your self-awareness? Take some time to contemplate these questions and explore the wisdom that can be found in the absence of sound.

READING #4:
IMAGES THAT PULL US FORWARD

In my various adventures, particularly the riskier ones, a single captivating image or vision has always fuelled me throughout the arduous months of preparation and eager anticipation. As I gear up for Pacific Solo, I find myself fixated on three particular images, each holding its own significance.

Firstly, I envision sailing out of Tokyo Bay, bidding farewell to my beloved family and friends, fully aware that I won't lay eyes on land or another soul for a gruelling stretch of two, possibly three, months. The mixed emotions of excitement and separation make this image a poignant reminder of the journey's magnitude.

Secondly, I had the compelling image or even vision of reaching English Bay in Vancouver, Canada, where my mother would be there to greet me. I moment where as a son I wanted to spring a smile of pride to my mother.

However, it is the third image that truly mesmerizes me: finding myself completely alone in the vastness of the North Pacific, gazing at the towering heights above and contemplating the unfathomable depths below. This image has consumed my thoughts and invaded my dreams. It has unveiled a revelation: my ultimate destination isn't Vancouver. Instead, it's precisely where this vision places me – in the heart of the Pacific at what I fondly call Nemo North, which, as I explained in Part One, is the spot in the North Pacific furthest from land in every direction.

While I have not yet reached the geographical location I have named Nemo North, I have in fact had Nemo North moments since leaving Tokyo on my voyage around Japan and have been enriched as a result. The image of being alone on the ocean in profound thought keeps me going back out to sea.

I encourage you to contemplate the power of images in your own life. Consider the visuals or visions that inspire you – the ones that ignite a sense of purpose or propel you forward. How do these images shape your aspirations and influence your choices? Take a moment to immerse yourself in the emotions evoked by these images and reflect on the significance they hold for you. What lessons can you glean from the images that draw you forward? Embrace the transformative potential of these visual inspirations as you navigate your own unique journey through life.

READING #5:
TIME TRAVEL

Ah, the passing of time, the inevitable march of age. We're all growing older, right? But here's the thing: while some may dread it, I find myself eagerly anticipating the future. Yes, I can already hear the naysayers admonishing me to live in the present. And I do! But you see, by keeping an eye on the future, I gain a heightened sensitivity and appreciation for the fleeting *now* moments.

Now, let's think about living in the moment. Truth be told, you can't really live in a moment because they are fleeting, here one second and gone the next. Time marches on relentlessly, sweeping us along for the ride.

But it's the future that captivates me. The distant horizon beckons, filled with the promise of discovery and enlightenment. However, it's more than just wonderment that stirs within me when I contemplate what lies ahead. I also feel a sense of guardianship over the time that I have at my disposal.

This sense of responsibility began for me when I read a book called *Future Shock* by Alvin Toffler.[22] His words profoundly influenced my thinking about the future. I still reflect on his use of the Barbie doll as a symbol of how rapidly the future is approaching, urging us to adapt and embrace change. And let's not forget *The 100-Year Life* by Lynda Gratton and Andrew Scott, which made me consider our longer lives not as merely consisting of growing older for longer but as an opportunity to stay younger for longer.[23] Such a refreshing perspective!

But what moves me more than anything is the fact that my grandson, and future generations, may live well beyond 100 years. This notion instils in me a tremendous sense of responsibility towards him and all those who will inhabit the 22nd century.

But what does all this have to do with my Pacific Solo adventure, you may wonder? To be honest, I'm not entirely certain I can articulate it just yet. But I can say this: there are things I wish to accomplish and a legacy I aspire to leave behind. Embarking on a solo voyage to the heart of the North Pacific is not merely an item on my bucket list; it is a profound quest for discovery and enlightenment.

Reflect on your own relationship with the future. How do you perceive the passing of time and the adventures that await? Do you share my enthusiasm for what lies ahead or does the thought of the future fill you with trepidation? Consider the legacy you wish to leave behind for future generations and the responsibility that comes with it. Take a moment to ponder, dream and embrace the exhilarating possibilities that the future holds.

READING #6:
MY TOP TEN FEARS (WHAT ARE YOURS?)

I am often asked whether I am scared to be at sea by myself. Yes, of course I am! After announcing my Pacific Solo challenge and being asked the question several times, I listed my top ten fears. Here they are in order from tenth to first.

#10: GOING UP
Scaling the mast for repairs used to send shivers down my spine. I have now discovered the mast climber, which enables me to climb the mast without the help of others. However, the thought of mast-climbing in the vast expanse of the Pacific still gives me a tinge of unease.

#9: GOING DOWN
The flip side of going up – plunging beneath the boat's surface to untangle debris or inspect hidden nooks. I haven't quite prepared for this feat, aside from pondering which equipment to use. There's an undeniable thrill in swimming and checking the boat, but what lurks in the deep depths below? Let's face it, the unknown can be quite chilling.

#8: STORMS

Navigating the tempestuous seas is no small feat. Staying on the sunny side of lows and the right side of highs is my quest. My voyage will take me through latitudes 35°–40°, in harmony with the prevailing winds. Armed with daily weather reports and advice from a brilliant meteorologist on land, I'll be ready to ride the waves.

#7: MECHANICAL REPAIRS

I'm no mechanical whiz, and understanding diesel engines is not my strength. More than once, my trusty mate Tony, a genius mechanic, and member of my shore team gave me a tutorial where he showed me the Top Ten Things that can go wrong with a diesel engine. He has responded to my emergency video call to help me solve a problem. Once was during a storm where if I did not find a repair to get my engine going again I would have possibly crashed into the rocks of a tiny island I needed to take refuge in.

#6: BEING ALONE

Ah, the solitude that beckons, both alluring and nerve-wracking. There are three dimensions to this fear. First, as a social butterfly, I'll undoubtedly miss my usual vibrant interactions with my family and friends. Second, the incessant worries about their well-being will nag at me. And then, there's the legendary 'solo sailor madness' that lurks in the depths and that I explored in Reading #3.

Yet, at the core, I fear the haunting memories of childhood nights spent trembling in fear of the dark. Will that fear resurface, amplified on the vast, lonely sea?

Nevertheless, amid the fear lies an irresistible allure – to embrace solitude in the heart of Nemo North and contemplate profound themes.

#5: HITTING SOMETHING

Ah, the perils that await! I have three particular concerns: navigating around other ships; ensuring the gentle giants of the sea (whales) are aware of my presence through acoustic signals; and the dreaded lurking containers that sit slightly submerged – a challenge beyond my control.

#4: FALLING OVERBOARD

I've established a golden rule: always be tethered when on deck and in the cockpit. No unplanned swimming adventures, unless I'm accompanied by the mischievous dolphins, of course!

#3: RUNNING OUT OF MONEY

Budgeting and financial planning have become the pillars of my voyage. With careful consideration and resourcefulness, and using many of the tips I've outlined in Part Three, I'll keep my dreams afloat.

#2: NOT GOING

Oh, how this fear once dominated my thoughts, lurking in the shadows. But, lo and behold, a shift occurred! The fear of *not* embarking on this grand adventure became greater than the fear of taking the leap.

#1: MY MOTHER

The greatest fear of all – an arrival too late, where my beloved mother won't recognize me. It weighs heavy on my heart. But I embark on this voyage not in haste, but with determination, thorough preparation and every ounce of courage I can muster. I shall set sail, aiming to reach my goal in due time!

What are your top ten fears, be they connected to your audacious dream or any other aspect of your life? Acknowledge them, embrace them and face them head on. For it is in confronting our fears that we discover the true depths of our strength and resilience. Let the adventure begin!

READING #7:
DEALING WITH CURVES AND CALAMITIES

Life is not a linear path; it is a winding adventure filled with unexpected curves and calamities. As we strive for our envisioned destinations, we must remember that change is inevitable.

A quote by Japanese theologian Kosuke Koyama captures this beautifully: "The womb is not a CUBE."[24] The womb, symbolizing the beginning of life, is fluid and flexible, just like life itself. We must be open and adaptable, embracing the momentum of new directions that unforeseen changes bring. Straight-line lives are stagnant and lack the vibrancy of the unexpected. It often takes a shock or surprise to liberate us from such a humdrum existence. Life's twists and turns, its entrances and exits, guide us towards new beginnings.

In times of crisis, we are reminded of the bedrock and ballast of our true values and sense of mission. These core beliefs become our anchor, grounding us when everything feels uncertain. They serve as a reminder of who we are and what we genuinely believe, beyond superficial words on a CV or in a corporate mission statement. Deeply held values provide the necessary weight to enable us to navigate troubled times, giving us a firm footing on the tumultuous journey.

Amid the challenges, it's crucial to seek inspiration and insight. Lift your eyes and gaze upon the distant horizon, where new possibilities await. The sight of these far-reaching goals can profoundly impact our ability to cope with the present, as we recognize that we are on a journey towards a better place. So, immerse yourself in stories and narratives of hope, allowing them to beckon you forward.

Let me share a personal experience. On 13 October 2019, at 5:10 am, I found myself on a boat braving Typhoon no. 19, also known as Hagibis. The intensity of the storm built up over hours, and then, following a particularly fierce 90 minutes, a moment of calm arrived. I now know that this was when the eye of the storm passed nearby. However, in the moment, I was uncertain as to where I was in relation to the storm, so I decided to close my eyes and seek respite in the land of dreams.

And I did find sleep. When I woke up hours later, I was greeted by a tranquil harbour, a star-studded sky above me. In that moment, I contemplated the lessons I had learned from this experience. There were the practical aspects of training, such as taking down and packing a jib, mastering essential knots and securing the boat with double moor lines. But the storm also reminded me of four profound life lessons.

First, during a storm, our world narrows down to the immediate time and space. It's a reminder to focus on the present moment, finding strength in the here and now.

Second, as the full fury of the storm unleashed upon my small ship, I realized that all the effort and preparation I had invested had not been in vain. The peace of mind that comes from readiness is invaluable.

Third, as in my experiences in war zones as part of my role heading up the non-profit HOPE, I was reminded that danger is a matter of proximity. A few metres can make all the difference between safety and vulnerability.

Lastly, I must emphasize the importance of living in hope. Faith is not merely passive endurance until the storm subsides; it is a spirit that carries us through, infused with fierce hope. As Corazon Aquino, former president of the Philippines and a woman I deeply respected, said after enduring her own storms, "Faith... is a spirit which bears things – with resignation, yes, but above all, with blazing serene hope."[25]

As you reflect on these musings, consider the curves and calamities you have encountered in your own journey. How have they shaped you? What are your bedrock values that keep you grounded? And where do you find inspiration and hope? May your reflections guide you towards embracing life's twists and turns with resilience and unwavering optimism.

READING #8 PERSEVERANCE: LESSONS FROM WINSTON CHURCHILL AND HOMER SIMPSON

"Gambatte kudasai" are words of encouragement spoken by Japanese pilgrims coming down Mount Fuji to those going up.

"Yeah, yeah, yeah," you may be thinking. "We all know that perseverance is important. Nothing new here."

But wait! Read on and hear me out. A lot has been written about perseverance (this was especially the case during the Covid-19 pandemic). But perhaps there is a nugget of truth to be found in these writings about the importance of enduring. Whether we face a self-imposed challenge or a crisis that has been inflicted on us, there is power to be found in perseverance. So read on. There are some lessons to be learned from Winston and Homer.

Over half a century ago, so the story goes, a plump man who had a liking for cigars and whisky shuffled to a podium to give an address. The speaker had achieved a lot – from mastering English as a failing student to showing courage throughout the Second World War, this man had demonstrated grit and determination. The students who gathered to hear him speak were in awe. The invited speaker leaned his cane against the podium, placed his top hat on a small table and took the cigar from his mouth, as he slowly rose onto his toes and leaned forward. Looking out over the great hall, he uttered three words, three times, each with a different emphasis:

NEVER give up.
Never give UP.
NEVER GIVE UP.

In actual fact, the speech was somewhat longer,[26] but this version is much better for my story! Of course, the message is nothing new. We have been told, often, that the 'tortoise wins the race.' It is the consistent, boring repetition of a task that achieves the desired goal. But it is not merely the achievement of the goal that is the reward of 'enduring.' There is something more – something spiritual and magical that happens when we press on. There is the potential of inner transformation, enlightenment and even epiphany. There is the potential of fog giving way to clarity. It may only be subtle, but incrementally, each time we take a step and action of perseverance, moving beyond our comfort zone and what we believe to be our personal limitation, we have the prospect of being rewarded by bluer skies, greener grass and a clearer vision of what can be.

In Japanese, the word for 'crisis' is composed of two Japanese characters. One means 'danger' while the meaning of the other is a blend of the two English words 'opportunity' and 'promise.' You see, any feat of endurance, whether physical, emotional, intellectual or even vocational, often involves a moment of crisis where you do not feel you can go on, and your body or mind says, "*No* more – that's enough!" Our 'being' is simply responding to its known limits based on past experience. Our inner self, our body, our mind is saying, "Any further is the unknown – are you sure you want to keep going?"

Homer Simpson has his own take on this concept and invented a word to describe it: "crisi-tinunity."[27] Every crisis carries both danger and the promise of an opportunity. Like an eagle rising on a thermal, you may discover a 'lift' that raises you to a new perspective on yourself and the possible paths forward.

Even when pain and crisis are inflicted on us by others or external forces, we still have a choice to move on, to survive and see a brighter day.

Here are some action points you may consider:

1. Be inspired! Read a book or watch a documentary about a person or community that survived and thrived after a calamity or challenge.
2. Reflect on your own life and remember the times when you felt an afterglow following a crisis or challenge. What did you learn?
3. Set short-term goals that will stretch and exercise the mental muscle you need to persevere. Use those accomplishments to pursue longer-term stretch goals.

FAIR WINDS

Congratulations! We have reached the final pages of *Dare to Dream*, where we can reflect on the incredible journey we've taken together – a journey of self-discovery, transformation and the pursuit of a life that aligns with our deepest aspirations. Starting with my "Memoirs of a Misfit Dreamer" (Part One) and the practical four-step programme for redesigning our lives (Part Two), we have explored the power of intention, the importance of mindset and tools we can use to navigate our unique paths (Part Three). Finally, we considered eight readings that can reinforce our determination and open our minds to new possibilities (Part Four). And now, as we stand at this crossroads, it is vital to recognize the significance of ambition and drive in creating a truly fulfilling and rewarding life.

Moving forward is all about taking incremental steps, and the first step need not be a daunting one (be sure to revisit the sections on navigating fear in Part Three). Allow me to share a personal experience that shaped my perspective on the importance of getting started. Years ago, I found myself facing a big book project. Although I had written several books before, I was struck by a bout of writer's block. It was during that time that I stumbled upon a quote widely (but probably apocryphally) attributed to Mark Twain that continues to guide me to this day. It says, "The secret of getting ahead is getting started! The key to getting started is breaking your complex, overwhelming tasks into small manageable ones and starting with the first one." This wisdom liberated me, reminding me to shift my focus from the road ahead and fix my gaze upon the very next step.

Another quote that continues to inspire me comes from the ancient Chinese philosopher Lao Tzu: "A journey of a thousand miles begins with one step."[28] You have already taken several steps to arrive here, and now it's time to forge ahead.

But why is it so crucial to dream big? The great artist Michelangelo is said to have once remarked, "The greater danger for most of us lies not in setting our aim too high and falling short; but in setting our aim too low, and achieving our mark." These words ring true, reminding us that playing it safe and settling for mediocrity can only lead to a life devoid of the extraordinary. We are meant to dream big, to stretch beyond our comfort zones and to reach for the stars with unwavering determination.

The poet T. S. Eliot echoed this sentiment when he asserted, "Only those who will risk going too far can possibly find out how far one can go."[29] Our capacity for growth and personal fulfilment is limited only by the boundaries we impose upon ourselves. It is through audacious endeavours and courageous leaps into the unknown that we truly discover our potential.

In fact, scientific research consistently demonstrates the profound impact of setting ambitious goals on our overall well-being. Such aspirations direct our attention, mobilize our efforts, increase our persistence and inspire the development of strategic plans. It is in the pursuit of these goals that our brain comes alive, activating both the amygdala, the centre of our emotions, and the frontal lobe, the problem-solving powerhouse that propels us forward.

Moreover, when we set goals that resonate with our deepest passions and ignite our emotional intensity, the obstacles and challenges that arise on our path lose their power. We become resilient in the face of adversity, undeterred by setbacks and unwavering in our commitment to realizing our dreams.

One remarkable study conducted at the University of Texas sheds light on the transformative effects of ambitious goal-setting. Even in the face of symptoms such as numbness, speech impairment, loss of muscular coordination and severe fatigue, individuals with multiple sclerosis who set ambitious wellness goals reported fewer and less severe symptoms. This research serves as a testament to the profound impact that daring to dream can have on our overall well-being and the resilience of the human spirit.[30]

So, dear reader, as we conclude this extraordinary journey together, I implore you to embrace the power of ambition. Let your dreams soar to breathtaking heights and have the courage to pursue them with unwavering determination. Trust in the remarkable capacity of your brain to adapt, to solve problems and to propel you towards the life you envision.

Remember, ambitious goals are not mere fantasies – they are brain-changers. They transform us, awaken our potential, and lead us to a life of purpose, fulfilment and unparalleled joy. You possess within you the strength, the resilience and the unwavering spirit to bring your dreams to life.

Now, my friend, it is time to leap forward with renewed vigour, armed with the knowledge, insights and tools you have acquired on this transformative journey. Embrace the boundless possibilities that await you, and let your ambitions shape the remarkable story of your life. Dare to dream, and dare to live a life that surpasses your wildest imagination.

Your time is now. Seize it, and may your dreams carry you to the distant horizons you were destined to reach.

Fair winds,
Lowell
Amami Oshima and on board sailing vessel *Wahine*

PS If you have not already done so, join me in the growing community of Never-Too-Laters at www.nevertoolateacademy.com, where together we can support and inspire each other.

NOTES

1. Oliver Burkeman, *Four Thousand Weeks: Time Management for Mortals* (New York: Farrar, Straus and Giroux, 2021).

2. Lowell Sheppard, *Chasing the Cherry Blossom: A Spiritual Journey through Japan* (Oxford: Lion, 2001).

3. Lowell Sheppard, *Boys Becoming Men: Creating Rites of Passage* (Carlisle: Authentic Lifestyle, 2002).

4. Lowell Sheppard, *Boys Becoming Men: Creating Rites of Passage* (Carlisle: Authentic Lifestyle, 2002).

5. Lowell Sheppard, *Boys Becoming Men: Creating Rites of Passage* (Carlisle: Authentic Lifestyle, 2002).

6. As described by the National Weather Service, "CAPE, or Convective Available Potential Energy, is the amount of fuel available to a developing thunderstorm. More specifically, it describes the instability of the atmosphere and provides an approximation of updraft strength within a thunderstorm." See "What Is Cape?" (National Weather Service), accessed 24 August 2023, https://www.weather.gov/ilx/swop-severetopics-CAPE.

7. Timothy Ferriss, *The 4-Hour Workweek: Escape the 9–5, Live Anywhere and Join the New Rich* (London: Vermillion, 2011).

8. Joseph Campbell quoted at "What We Are Really Living for..." (Joseph Campbell Foundation), accessed 26 August 2023, https://jcf.org/quote/what-we-are-really-living-for-is-the-experience-of-life-both-the-pain.

9. Gail Saltz, *The Power of Different: Genius and the Link between Disorder and Extraordinary Ability* (London: Robinson, 2017).

10. Joseph Campbell quoted at "What We Are Really Living for…" (Joseph Campbell Foundation), accessed 26 August 2023, https://jcf.org/quote/what-we-are-really-living-for-is-the-experience-of-life-both-the-pain.

11. Xavier de Maistre, *Voyage Around My Room* (Sardinia: Aturin, 1794).

12. C. S. Lewis, *Surprised by Joy: The Shape of My Early Life* (London: Geoffrey Bles, 1955).

13. Lowell Sheppard, *Boys Becoming Men: Creating Rites of Passage* (Carlisle: Authentic Lifestyle, 2002).

14. Kathleen Norris, *The Cloister Walk* (New York: Riverhead, 1996).

15. A modern edition is Inazō Nitobe, *Bushido: The Soul of Japan* (London: Penguin Books, 2002).

16. Lowell Sheppard, *Never Too Late: Ten Tips for Changing the Course of Your Life* (Oxford: Monarch, 2005).

17. John Kretschmer, *Sailing to the Edge of Time* (London: Adlard Coles Nautical, 2019).

18. Vito Dumas, *Alone through the Roaring Forties* (London: Adlard Coles Nautical, 1960).

19. 'Silence on the Surf', 2019, Pacific Solo Blog https://www.pacificsolo.com/blog/2019/silence-and-solitude

20. 'Silence on the Surf', (Ibid).

21. Xavier de Maistre, *Voyage Around My Room* (Ibid).

22. Alvin Toffler, *Future Shock* (New York: Random House, 1970).

23. Lynda Gratton and Andrew Scott, *The 100-Year Life: Living and Working in an Age of Longevity* (London: Bloomsbury Business, 2017).

24. Kosuke Koyama, *Three Mile an Hour God*, (New York: Orbis Books, 1980).

25. Corazon Aquino quoted at "Woman of the Year" (*Time*), last modified 5 January 1987, https://content.time.com/time/subscriber/article/0,33009,963185-9,00.html.

26. America's National Churchill Museum | Never Give In, Never, Never, Never

27. "Fear of Flying," season 6, episode 11 of *The Simpson* (Gracie Films and 20th Television).

28. Lao Tzu, *Dao De Jing*, chapter 64.

29. T. S. Eliot, preface to Harry Crosby, *The Transit of Venus* (Paris: Black Sun Press, 1931).

30. Alexa K. Stuifbergen, Heather Becker, Gayle M. Timmerman and Vicki Kullberg, "The Use of Individualized Goal Setting to Facilitate Behavior Change in Women with Multiple Sclerosis," *Journal of Neuroscience* 35, no. 2 (2003): 94–96.

ACKNOWLEDGEMENTS

In the journey of bringing this book to life, I am profoundly grateful for the unwavering support of many.

My heartfelt appreciation goes to the co-founders of the Never Too Late Academy (NTLA): Mike Alfant, Paul Dupuis, Harry Hill, Doug Hymas, Mark McBennet, Kush Mirchandani, Mackenzie Sheppard, and Ryan Sheppard, who, in their own unique ways, have championed this endeavor. Special recognition also extends to Steve Houck, a pivotal force in the inception of NTLA. And to the NTLA team past and present who contributed to creation of the academy and this book. Brent Sheppard, Bruce McCaughan, Joshua Collard, Carter Witt, and Estaban Moralomonte, your encouragement and input have significantly shaped the content within these pages.

A big thank you to Martin Liu and the entire team at LID Publishing, whose steadfast support, diligent editing by Clare with the assistance of Hazel, and Teya's support in releasing the book have been instrumental.

I also am profoundly grateful to John Flanagan, Chris Humphries, Yuji Ueda, and the entire History Channel team for their belief in the importance of sharing the story of "Dare to Dream."

Special thanks to Matt Pride and MitsuHaru Kume for their rapid response in printing the book proofs and delivering them to my hospital room on Amami Island within a few hours. Mitsu even managed to sneak in a few snacks. Thank you.

And last but never least, my family: Kande, Ryan, Mac, Eli, Maria, and Hitomi in Japan, along with all my relatives. To my late mother, who was herself an author and assisted with wordcraft on my previous books, thank you, mother.

This book is a testament to the power of collective vision, dedication, and unwavering belief. To all those named and unnamed, your faith and encouragement have fueled my journey.

Note: I would also like to acknowledge the invaluable role played by all of my Pacific Solo Sponsors, Patrons, Shore team, Boat Search Team, supporters on Kickstarter and GoFundMe, along with all my YouTube Followers, in making my dream a reality. You can find a complete list of their names on www.pacificsolo.com and the Pacific Solo YouTube Channel.

Thank you all for being part of this incredible journey.